Differentiated science teaching

DEVELOPING SCIENCE AND TECHNOLOGY EDUCATION

Series Editor: Brian Woolnough
Department of Educational Studies, University of Oxford

Differentiated science teaching

RESPONDING TO INDIVIDUAL DIFFERENCES
AND TO SPECIAL EDUCATIONAL NEEDS

KEITH POSTLETHWAITE

Open University Press
Buckingham · Philadelphia

Open University Press
Celtic Court
22 Ballmoor
Buckingham
MK18 1XW

and
1900 Frost Road, Suite 101
Bristol, PA 19007, USA

First published 1993
Reprinted 1996

A catalogue record of this book is available from the British Library

Library of Congress Cataloging-in-Publication Data

Postlethwaite, Keith.
    Differentiated science teaching: responding to individual
differences and to special education needs / Keith Postlethwaite.
        p.   cm.
    Includes bibliographical references and index.
    ISBN 0–335–15707–6   ISBN 0–335–15706–8 (pbk.)
    1. Science—Study and teaching.   2. Differentiated teaching
staff.   3. Differentiation (Developmental psychology)   I. Title.
Q181.P495   1993
507.1′2—dc20   92–20523
                                                                    CIP

Typeset by Graphicraft Typesetters Ltd., Hong Kong
Printed in Great Britain by St Edmundsbury Press Limited
Bury St Edmunds, Suffolk

To my mother

who has taught me the respect for individuals
on which my professional interest in
differentiation is based

Contents

Series editor's preface

It may seem surprising that after three decades of curriculum innovation, and with the increasing provision of centralised National Curriculum, that it is felt necessary to produce a series of books which encourage teachers and curriculum developers to continue to rethink how science and technology should be taught in schools. But teaching can never be merely the 'delivery' of someone else's 'given' curriculum. It is essentially a personal and professional business in which lively, thinking, enthusiastic teachers continue to analyse their own activities and mediate the curriculum framework to their students. If teachers ever cease to be critical of what they are doing then their teaching, and their students' learning, will become sterile.

There are still important questions which need to be addressed, questions which remain fundamental but the answers to which may vary according to the social conditions and educational priorities at a particular time.

What is the justification for teaching science and technology in our schools? For educational or vocational reasons? Providing science and technology for all, for future educated citizens, or to provide adequately prepared and motivated students to fulfil the industrial needs of the country? Will the same type of curriculum satisfactorily meet both needs or do we need a differentiated curriculum? In the past it has too readily been assumed that one type of science will meet all needs.

What should be the nature of science and technology in schools? It will need to develop both the methods and the content of the subject, the way a scientist or engineer works and the appropriate knowledge and understanding, but what is the relationship between the two? How does the student's explicit knowledge relate to investigational skill, how important is the student's tacit knowledge? In the past the holistic nature of scientific activity and the importance of affective factors such as commitment and enjoyment have been seriously undervalued in relation to the student's success.

And, of particular concern to this series, what is the relationship between science and technology? In some countries the scientific nature of technology and the technological aspects of science make the subjects a natural continuum. In others the curriculum structures have separated the two leaving the teachers to develop appropriate links. Underlying this series is the belief that science and technology have an important interdependence and thus many of the books will be appropriate to teachers of both science and technology.

Keith Postlethwaite's book will be a stimulus to anyone concerned that each student should develop their potential in the science lessons. It is not primarily about organisational strategies, or even about what a teacher should do – though there are many important guidelines included. It is primarily about gaining an understanding of individual students, how they think and how they learn, and thus developing attitudes towards students so that the learning experience matches their potential. It is an optimistic book, asserting that nearly all students can master the content and processes of science if taught appropriately and uses Blooms' theory of mastery learning as one way. The book nicely intertwines theory and practice, asserting that successful practice can only be developed by teachers as they actively engage with underlying theory. Any teacher concerned with issues of differentiation or of special needs will find much of value here.

Brian E. Woolnough

Acknowledgements

One of the most pleasant aspects of writing a book is to produce the acknowledgements, as the process encourages the author to think back over the wide range of support, help and friendship which has contributed to its production. In my case, in relation to this book, this has been a particularly pleasant activity.

The book has been greatly influenced by two groups of people. The first were those with whom I worked at the University of Oxford Department of Educational Studies. I learnt a great deal from all my colleagues there, but am particularly indebted to Donald McIntyre who helped me to move forward from some very preliminary ideas to the more developed approach which I have tried to summarise in the pages that follow. I would also like to pay tribute to Ann Hackney, James Gray, Bridie Raban and Cliff Denton with whom I worked on various research projects on topics related to the book. Under Harry Judge's inspiring leadership, this department and this group of people were a very important influence on the ideas which make up this book.

The second major source of influence has been my present group of colleagues in the Faculty of Education and Community Studies at Reading University. The book is closely related to an MSc course which I give there. Its director, David Malvern, has been a constant source of ideas and encouragement; its students, mainly from the UK and Africa, but also from places as far apart as Ireland and Japan, have forced me to clarify much of my thinking and have contributed a great deal to the shape of the text. The students' enquiring approach, their determination to understand how ideas can be applied in their often very different contexts, and their energy and enthusiasm have all been a significant influence. I can only apologise to those who suffered the earliest versions of the course, and therefore had to try to make sense of the material in an even less developed form!

Some of the ideas of the book have also been explored with PGCE science students at Reading. My colleagues Chris Gayford, David Reynolds and John Gilbert have therefore had a considerable influence on what appears below. In particular, David Reynolds and I were involved in a two-year research project on TVEI in Initial Teacher Education through which the mastery learning materials (see Chapter 4, and Appendices 1 and 2) were developed and evaluated. This work was done in cooperation with experienced teachers Jenny Morgan and John Perkins, industrial consultant Mike Brophy, and student teachers Sandy Pearce, Elaine Evans and Gillian Hetherington, to all of whom I owe a great deal.

During the writing of the book, I was fortunate to spend some time at Chiltern Edge School working with Sue Cane, Sally Harris and Rod Mantell. I very much appreciate their time, their ideas and the way in which they gave me access to their school and their classes. The experience, as well as being enjoyable, helped me to focus some of my ideas and reinforced my belief in the tremendous professionalism with which teachers tackle the complex issues that the text is concerned with. To them, their colleagues and their pupils I am most grateful.

It has been my particular good fortune that all these colleagues have not only contributed widely and generously to the ideas in the text, but that they have also provided me with much valued friendship. Though the book benefits greatly from their influence, I have not discussed the details of the text with them. I would therefore like to emphasise that they carry no responsibility for its shortcomings, though they certainly deserve credit for any successes.

One of my Oxford colleagues deserves special mention: Brian Woolnough has been a splendid editor who has managed to offer thoughtful comment on drafts of the material even though they were submitted perilously close to deadlines. Such clarity as the text possesses owes much to Brian's skill and understanding.

Thanks are also clearly due to the staff of Open University Press who, like Brian, have had to cope with my difficulties over deadlines. They have always responded with more understanding than I deserve.

Finally, I would like to acknowledge the support which I have been given by my wife, Kathryn. Her acceptance of the extent to which I have left so many day to day things to her has been a great help. However, of greater significance are the high standards which she sets in her own professional life, for I continually find these to be genuinely inspiring.

CHAPTER 1

Introductions

An introduction to the field

Children differ from one another in a great variety of ways, many of which are relevant to their work as pupils in school. Children with special educational needs are part of this continuum of variation, but they lie towards an extreme of one or more of the dimensions of that variation. Clearly, if the educational system is to serve all these different children well, including those with special needs, it must consider how to respond to the relevant differences, and to what ends this response should be directed. The present book is concerned with selected aspects of this debate. It discusses ways in which teachers in mainstream secondary schools can help all their pupils benefit, to the greatest extent to which they are capable, from a common science curriculum.

The previous sentence is an important one. It encapsulates many of the starting points for this book. I shall therefore begin by considering it carefully. I shall first make brief reference to all the points it makes, and then return to two in greater detail.

A crucial point is the emphasis on *teachers*. I shall argue that the most significant response of the education system to the wide range of pupils with which it works is not one of large-scale system organisation (such as provision of selective schools and special schools), nor one of individual school organisation (such as use of setting or streaming), but one of imaginative and flexible teaching on the part of teachers. In relation to the science curriculum, mainstream science teachers and special needs teachers will each have a role to play, but, it is undoubtedly these teachers, not politicians or administrators, who will create solutions to the complex question of responding effectively to all children in school.

The emphasis on pupils in *mainstream* schools serves to flag that this book is not concerned with the highly specialised task of teaching pupils with the most severe educational disabilities. Even in systems which stress integration, such pupils are still very rarely found in mainstream schools – even at the level of locational integration.

The emphasis on *science* is a consequence of two things: first, it reflects my general belief that the most helpful books on the subject of attending to differences amongst pupils are likely to be those which concentrate on one subject area so that examples can be explored in sufficient depth to be of direct relevance to a teacher's teaching; secondly, it is a consequence of the fact that my own professional background is in science teaching.

The emphasis on *secondary* schools is less fundamental. My own teaching experience is at this level and examples from this context fall most readily and most convincingly to hand. However, the subject oriented specification of the UK National Curriculum for primary as well as secondary stages suggests that some of what this book has to say about responding to individual differences amongst pupils in a subject teaching context may also have relevance to primary teachers.

Perhaps the most important single point in that earlier sentence is its emphasis on *all* pupils. The book does deal with the teaching of science to pupils who have special educational needs, though within that large field it will concentrate on pupils with learning difficulties or high ability. However, a fundamental stance of the book is that the tactics which a teacher might use to make provision for such pupils are unlikely to be effective if they are considered in isolation from the broader teaching strategies which are adopted for all the pupils in the class. The book is therefore about differentiation in the teaching of science to all pupils, including those with special educational needs.

Differentiation for all can clearly be justified in its own terms. It seems to me self evident that, if we require all pupils to attend school from the age of 5 to the age of 16, then we have a professional duty to ensure that what is offered in school is relevant to each of those pupils. This is one of the ways in which a school teacher differs from, say, a person running a voluntary evening class. In the latter context the teacher can reasonably say: 'This is what I shall do and how I shall do it. Take it if it suits you, or leave it if it does not.' Since in formal schooling the pupils cannot 'leave it', it follows that the teacher should not adopt teaching styles which are inaccessible to any of the individuals who have to 'take it'. Indeed if we were to announce openly that it was our intention to teach to one particular level and that other pupils would simply have to sink or swim, it would not only offend against natural justice but would also be quite unacceptable to pupils and their parents. This case for the teacher needing to take account of differentiation for all is further strengthened by the fact that differentiation is a clear element of national policy which runs through the DES policy statements of the mid-1980s, the GCSE criteria, the National Curriculum and the concerns of CATE (the body which accredits courses of initial teacher education).

The arguments of principle and policy rehearsed above clearly apply to pupils with special needs who should therefore be included in the scope of any differentiation we are planning. However, the importance of provision for such pupils being

related to an *overall* policy of differentiation became clarified for me during a research project on the effectiveness of enrichment materials for able pupils in which I was involved. One, almost incidental, finding of that research was that the teachers who thought about varied provision for all pupils in their classes found it possible to help able pupils use enrichment materials in an effective manner. Those for whom provision for the able was seen as something to be grafted on to an otherwise homogeneous teaching style reported much more difficulty in achieving this end. My confidence in the validity of the view that general differentiation was a significant factor in special needs provision was greatly reinforced by the ideas of John Fish (1985) which were expressed in his important book *Special Education: The Way Ahead*. Fish argued that (p. 26):

> A search for higher standards and more effective schools has implications for special education. These depend on how the search is carried out. On the one hand, it could result in a better matching of tasks, objectives and materials to individuals. On the other, it could result in a narrower common curriculum, a less flexible approach to individual needs and the stigmatisation of pupils as not up to standard. The former approach leads to special educational arrangements being seen as a variant of a number of different approaches to learning while the latter may characterise it as charitable provision for failures.

This convinced me that to consider differentiated teaching for all pupils is not to marginalise the issue of provision for pupils with special needs. Rather it is to face that issue head on, in an admittedly complex framework, but one which cannot be ignored if effective provision for pupils with special needs is to be made.

Finally, that earlier key sentence talks about helping pupils to benefit, to the greatest extent to which they are capable, *from a common science curriculum*. The Warnock Report (HMSO, 1978) made a strong case that education for children with special needs should itself be special, not in terms of the aims or objectives which it sets for pupils, but in terms of the methods it uses to help all pupils towards common, socially valued goals. This can also be seen as a significant strand in curriculum documents in the 1980s and in the National Curriculum in England and Wales (though recent developments (e.g. in relation to music) could be said to have challenged this position to some extent). The arguments for this focus on a common curriculum have been summarised elsewhere (e.g. Postlethwaite and Hackney, 1988) and I refer to one significant argument at the start of Chapter 3.

The phrase about pupils benefitting *'to the greatest extent to which they are capable'* is a recognition that some pupils will move more slowly through any common curriculum than others. It is important that the teacher does not have predetermined limits in mind for any individual pupil – whether they be fast working, able or motivated pupils, or slower, less able or less motivated pupils. But it is also important that we avoid the trap of aiming for exactly the same achievements for everyone within a fixed period of schooling, for that would be either to impose artificial limits on the attainments of some pupils or to make unrealistic demands on others. In Chapter 4, I shall discuss a model of teaching which addresses these issues by enabling all pupils to work for mastery of a common core curriculum while allowing opportunities for some to explore significant objectives outside this common core.

I hope that the book will be helpful to teachers, to student teachers and to those who provide initial teacher education. Perhaps it will also be of interest to parents, governors and administrators who help to determine the circumstances in which these professional educators work. It is, though, important for all these readers to remember that no book of this kind can provide ready-made solutions for teachers to apply in their own teaching. What it can do is refocus teachers' thinking, encourage critical examination of their current practice, extend the range of possible solutions which they are aware of, and stimulate their own creative responses to the particular set of opportunities and constraints within which they work.

Before embarking on the main part of the book, it may be helpful to say a little more about some of the points raised above and to introduce a further general consideration. First, it is interesting to consider in a little more detail how the debate about the way in which the educational system should respond to differences amongst pupils has changed its focus over time. Certainly, there do seem to have been significant changes in the dominant formulation of that debate. It would be wrong, of course, to suggest that all teachers, all schools or even all LEAs have kept in step with the 'majority position'. Some have held on to formulations which were at the heart of earlier debates; others have been instrumental in challenging accepted thinking and have been the stimulus which has taken the dominant view forward. However, despite these important variations, the changes in the main focus of the debate are of interest.

For many years after the Education Act 1944, the issue of how to respond to differences amongst pupils was considered to be an institutional matter. It was seen as a question of selecting supposedly different types of pupil for different types of school – for grammar schools, or for secondary modern schools, or for special schools. The validity of this model is questionable. For example, it is interesting to note that, after the development of comprehensive schooling, research which compared comprehensive and selective systems failed consistently to establish that selection produced higher overall levels of attainment (Clifford and Heath, 1984).

Within comprehensive schools themselves, the debate shifted to one about organisation. It was then more often formulated in terms of the suspected problems and proposed merits of separating the wide range of pupils in a given school into different streams or ability sets, or of placing them in mixed-ability groups. Interestingly, research comparing grouping systems seemed, like the research on selective schooling, to be dominated by findings of 'no significant difference' (Newbold, 1977; Postlethwaite and Denton, 1978). There was again no clear evidence that any one of these organisational strategies, in itself, held the solution to higher standards of education for all pupils.

Most recently, the dominant professional concern has been changing again, away from group-based institutional and organisational procedures and towards notions of how, through appropriate teaching, individual pupils' needs can be most adequately catered for within a comprehensive school, and within whatever grouping system has been adopted by that school.

The place of pupils with special needs in these different strategies is interesting. In selective schooling, and in the early years of mixed-ability grouping, special schools were seen to be appropriate for the 2 per cent or so of pupils with the most significant difficulties. A larger group of less disadvantaged pupils (up to 20 per cent of the school population) were placed in the mainstream system and, for them, special classes, small 're-medial sets' or withdrawal systems were seen as the appropriate approach. Thus, in various ways, pupils with special needs were usually taught outside the system that was regarded as appropriate for most other pupils. Post-Warnock, thinking has changed. Although pupils with the most severe educational disabilities are still usually placed in special schools, many pupils with quite significant difficulties are now integrated into mainstream schools, and into mainstream classes within those schools, despite disabilities which would earlier have placed them within the special school sector (Postlethwaite and Hackney, 1988). Provision for them then becomes a matter for the teacher of those classes, with support from special needs specialists based in the school or elsewhere within the LEA. For most of the 20 per cent group generally regarded as having special educational needs who have always been educated in mainstream schools, systems involving separate classes or withdrawal are tending to be replaced or supplemented by systems in which pupils are educated in mainstream classes (Postlethwaite and Hackney, 1988). Again, provision falls to the mainstream teacher, sometimes with the support of special needs staff or of non-teaching assistants.

Professional pressure is therefore towards differentiated approaches to the teaching of all pupils – hence the focus of this book. As *political* pressure in the UK begins to refocus attention on grouping systems, it will be important for professional educators to remember that such systems, in themselves, have not provided solutions in the past. A given grouping system *may* make it easier for a teacher to respond to individual differences, but it is only if we maintain an interest in the differentiation of teaching within whatever grouping system we operate that we can hold out hope of avoiding a return to sterile, over-simplistic 'solutions' to what is undoubtedly a complex pedagogic problem.

An important factor in the changes mapped above has been the change in emphasis from responses built around notions of differences amongst groups of pupils, to those designed around individual differences. Institutional and organisational responses to pupil differences are clearly consistent with a belief that the differences that matter are essentially those amongst groups of pupils – groups which can be conveniently identified and then assigned to the different schools or streams. More recent thinking stresses the characteristics of the individual pupil and the consequent response which the teacher must make to that individual (albeit in a class context). This is an interesting issue which deserves some further consideration as it would be easy to give the seriously misleading message that concern about groups is, in some sense, wrong.

In some contexts it is essential to think about group differences: for example, when considering differences of race, or gender, or social class. Such group differences are characterised by the fact that, in each case, large numbers of pupils fall into each of a relatively small group of categories. Pupils in each of these categories may have, or may be perceived to have, different educational needs; they may make, or may be expected to make, different responses to educational provision. What is more, these needs and responses may be significantly influenced by the status of the group in society as a whole and by the attitudes of society to the group. The group is therefore an important factor which must be taken into account in planning provision for all the pupils in that group. To ignore the role of the group can lead to inappropriate attitudes and actions. For example, educational decision makers should not expect teachers fully to remedy the under-performance of some girls in science by addressing individual learning needs, unless the system is also doing something to change sexist attitudes and stereo-typed expectations and role models within society generally. An individual girl's under-performance may be affected by individual characteristics which the teacher can understand and address by responding to her individual learning needs, but it may also be affected by factors which arise because she is a member of the group 'girls' which generates expectations, attitudes and opportunities which can only be addressed in relation to that group as a whole (and then only in part by the teacher in their role as teacher).

Group-based decision making therefore has an important place, but not all differences amongst pupils can properly be thought of as group differences. Some can best be thought of as individual differences: for example, differences in ability, or motivation, or prior learning, or alternative framework. Groups or categories are less important here. It is the difference between one individual and another that is significant. These differences can be quantitative (e.g. differences in the extent to which pupils have a particular characteristic such as IQ; or they may be qualitative, e.g. differences in the nature of pupils' naïve understanding of a scientific concept).

What is interesting in the context of this book is that ability, an individual difference and not a group difference, was so often the basis of institutional or organisational decisions about pupils' educational futures. Placing pupils in different schools, or different sets or streams necessarily assumes that groups of pupils should be treated differently. Of course, there are really no neat categories of IQ that can then be made to correspond to a neat set of school types. Furthermore, once one recognises that qualitative differences in understanding can be at least as significant as quantitative IQ differences, the search for a neat set of types of school, or of streams or bands within a school, looks much less than wise. Therefore, ability-based grouping decisions on school placement or streaming could only be expected to lead

to acceptable educational outcomes if attention was also paid to individual differences within the groups. Unfortunately, this was not a strong feature of that thinking. Top sets were (probably) taught differently from bottom sets, grammar school pupils were (probably) taught differently from pupils in secondary modern schools, but individual differences within a set or a grammar school were not a major feature of the planning or practice. As a result, the decision-making risked falling into the trap of stereotyping which is always present if emphasis is placed on group differences. The trap is that characteristics of a given category of pupils (both characteristics that are firmly established by careful research, and those which arise from common experience, suspicion, or hearsay) may be applied in an over-generalised way to all individuals in that category, and that insufficient attention may then be paid to the individual differences amongst the pupils in that category. Inappropriate educational provision, or expectations, or responses can then follow for an individual pupil as a result of these stereotypical views.

The change in emphasis to planning on the basis of individual difference is an attempt to get over many of the problems associated with this inappropriate use of group-based decision making. However, the change does bring its own risks. One has already been raised: namely, that if we view all educational needs on an individual basis, we may begin to pay too little attention to the effects of the status in society of the groups to which a pupil belongs. Just as group-based decisions can only function effectively if individual decisions are superimposed, so the converse may also prove to be true. This is something which needs further exploration. Solutions may lie largely outside practice in the classroom and are certainly outside the scope of this book. However, it is necessary to raise the point if we are not to be presented, as teachers, with an impossible task and then condemned for failing to achieve it.

In the classroom context, the idea of truly individual differences presents teachers with several very challenging problems which are properly our professional concern. For example, how are we to make accurate and sufficiently broad assessments of each pupil in order to respond appropriately to their different needs, and having made such assessments, how are we to manage our responses given the resources available, and the expectations of pupils, parents, school governors and governments with respect to what education in schools should be like? Also, in relation to pupils with special educational needs, the emphasis on individual differences is a timely reminder that although it might be valuable to talk about children with, say, moderate learning difficulties in a general way in book such as this, at the level of provision in the classroom, generalities have to be replaced with careful individual assessment and provision.

In summary, thinking about the differences amongst pupils has shifted from group-based differences towards individual differences and from broad institutional and organisational approaches to what the teacher actually does in the classroom. It is this emphasis on classroom teaching in response to individual differences in mainstream schools that is the concern of this book. This does not negate the importance of considering the groups to which pupils may belong, nor of pursuing responses to educational difficulties outside the narrow context of the classroom or school. It is simply that these are not issues dealt with at length here.

An introduction to the layout of the book

After the brief introduction provided by the present chapter, Chapter 2 is concerned with a more detailed look at general principles. It will provide an analysis of the nature of individual differences which might be relevant to the science teacher. By drawing on, and expanding, ideas that have been developed in an earlier article (McIntyre and Postlethwaite, 1989) it will identify various kinds of difference and the characteristics of each. In relation to the most significant of these (educational and psychological differences), it will outline relevant research findings to give a general picture of the characteristics of pupils which

are relevant to their learning of science. It will include discussion of what the particular characteristics of pupils with special educational needs might be. One outcome of the analysis in this chapter is that simplistic division of pupils into a small number of types of school, or into just ability groups within a school can never be a full response to the issue of individual pupils' needs. Another implication is that we should be willing to think of responses of two kinds: *remedial responses* in which we attempt to alter some aspect of the pupil and *circumvention responses* in which we seek to help pupils despite some continuing characteristics that might otherwise impede their learning.

Chapter 3 is concerned with specific remedial and circumvention tactics which an individual teacher might deploy to help pupils who find science difficult to learn, and to extend and enrich the science education of those who learn it with ease. It relates these tactics to the analysis of the range of pupil characteristics that were discussed in Chapter 2. It is a long chapter, but is divided into two major sections: one is concerned with tactics relevant to educational differences amongst pupils; the other deals with tactics which address psychological differences. The chapter outlines the theoretical and empirical background of these tactics and provides examples of their application to science teaching, basing illustrations on content which can be easily linked to the National Curriculum.

The development of such tactics is a challenging task for the teacher, but it is perhaps the easy part of making provision for the whole range of our pupils, including those with special educational needs. An even more difficult issue is that of how to bring tactics into play in the complex context of a busy laboratory or classroom. Chapter 4 is about this issue. Several strategies which the individual teacher can use are discussed, again at the level of principle as well as day-to-day practice. However, the particular emphasis of this chapter is on Bloom's Mastery Learning model which will be illustrated through an example which I developed with several lecturer, teacher and student teacher colleagues in Reading. Since the range of pupils in mainstream schools is becoming ever broader, this section also looks beyond the resources of the individual teacher in supporting pupils with special educational needs and discusses ways in which the relationship between the science teacher and the special needs department can be managed to provide appropriate support.

Finally, in Chapter 5, I will discuss the role of theory (of the kinds described elsewhere in the book) in influencing teachers' practice. I hope that, by providing specific examples of tactics for the more able, of tactics for pupils with learning difficulties, and of more general classroom strategies, the book will directly help teachers to extend their repertoire of action in the classroom. More importantly, I hope that by relating these ideas to broad theoretical frameworks, the book will encourage teachers to consider ways of modifying the suggested approaches to suit their own national or local situations, without losing sight of the relevant principles. The emphasis of this chapter is therefore on the essential part that teachers have to play in *creating* solutions to the problems of differentiated teaching that are appropriate to their own professional context.

Any book of this kind has to be selective in its content. The principle which has guided selection in this case is that change in provision in schools rests on teacher attitudes towards the differences amongst pupils, and teacher knowledge of appropriate tactics and strategies for responding to such differences. I hope that Chapters 3 and 4 will have some direct effect in broadening teachers' repertoire of tactics and strategies; I hope that these chapters, together with the more general context provided by Chapters 2 and 5, will have some influence on attitudes.

As emphasised in Chapter 5, I do not pretend that this book provides ready-made answers. However, I hope that it will stimulate enquiry on the part of teachers. This may be informal trial of individual tactics, or a full-scale action research study of a teaching strategy, or something between these two extremes. It is through such enquiry that teachers will construct their own understanding and develop their own skills, in ways that are sensitive to general principles and to the particular contexts of their own schools. I acknowledge that this process is demanding at a time when so many demands are placed on teachers' time and energy. I would argue, however, that there is no alternative – that professional development can never be handed over through a lecture, or course, or book, that it has to be constructed in context. I am confident that teachers will want to engage in the process.

CHAPTER 2

Different pupils, different responses

The focus

This book addresses the question of how science teachers in mainstream secondary schools can meet the educational needs of all their pupils. It therefore parallels the emphasis on differentiating teaching to match the characteristics of individual pupils which is apparent in much of the recent educational change in England and Wales. This emphasis can be traced through numerous HMI reports (e.g. HMI, 1978, 1979, 1982), through policy documents such as 'Science 5–16' (DES and Welsh Office, 1985b), through the concern over differentiation in the GCSE criteria (DES and Welsh Office, 1985a), through much of the background to the National Curriculum (e.g. DES and Welsh Office, 1989a; NCC, 1989a,b 1991), through the TVEI initiative (DES and Welsh Office, 1991a) and through the criteria of the Council for the Accreditation of Teacher Education (DES and Welsh Office, 1989c).

Throughout, and especially in Chapter 3, I shall be directly concerned with those pupils whose educational needs are sufficiently extreme or unusual to be designated 'special' but I will argue that these special needs can best be met when a general concern for individual differences is uppermost in teachers' thinking. However, I will not deal with pupils with the most severe educational disabilities such as the profoundly and multiply handicapped who are, at present, very rarely found in mainstream schools. Also, within the special needs field, I shall be particularly concerned with learning difficulties and with high ability. This is not completely to exclude pupils who have medical conditions, or physical or sensory handicaps: it is merely to focus on trying to understand and respond to the learning difficulties and the learning opportunities that may be associated with their conditions. Nor is it to exclude pupils who have behavioural difficulties: again it is to focus on the consequences for learning which follow from the behavioural repertoire which they adopt. In short, with regard to these sub-groups of pupils within the special needs field, the book is concerned with enhancing learning and not with means of dealing directly with the physical or medical condition in the classroom, or of managing the disruptive behaviour as such. These are admittedly highly arbitrary limitations. The teacher has to deal with pupils as complete individuals and, in practice, cannot choose to attend to just one aspect of their individuality. Nevertheless, I hope that the book will be helpful in the area which it addresses, and that teachers will find that it supplements other texts (e.g. Male and Thompson, 1985; Gray and Richer, 1988) which deal with the areas which are not covered here.

Before we can seriously consider ways in which we might respond, as science teachers, to the individual differences amongst our pupils, and especially to those differences which relate to learning, we should take time to analyse exactly how pupils differ. That is the purpose of the present chapter.

Kinds of differences amongst pupils

At an anecdotal level we can quickly convince ourselves that there are differences of many kinds. In a class of 12-year olds, Lucy was quite capable of discussing possible causes of pollution, but revealed that she had no understanding of the concept of 'between'. 'The factory is between the two towns' had no meaning for her. I wondered how much of our lessons passed her by and marvelled at the fact that she had acquired so much understanding in spite of her patchwork of basic concepts. Michael was short of confidence and spent most of the time allocated for a test doing immaculate drawings in answer to the first question rather than risking his hand at later questions which he felt he might not be able to do. I was as surprised as he was at what he could actually achieve when given sufficient support to risk the attempt, and was concerned that it was so difficult to spend enough time with him to help him at the appropriate moment. Graham was full of good scientific ideas which he could communicate very clearly when he spoke about them, but his written work was slow and laboured, his spelling was chaotic and he quickly lost interest when required to write his ideas down. I wondered whether, at 15, he would still be willing to engage in lessons or whether assessments based so much on written work would have succeeded in fooling him (and us) into thinking that he was not really very good at science. John's writing was so large that it was impossible for him to draw up a table or label a diagram since he could never fit what he wanted to write into the space available. The difficulty with diagrams was a nuisance, but the problem with tables meant that he was not really getting a sense of how useful they could be as a means of recording and communicating information.

At the same time, in a different class of 13-year olds, Sarah was able to predict, entirely on her own initiative, that reversing the current in a motor effect experiment must reverse the force on the wire carrying that current. She had already shown by experiment that reversing the magnetic field reversed the force, and she recognised that reversing the current was the topological equivalent of reversing the field. Her argument is summarised in Figure 2.1. Even to those who do not recognise the physics, the abstract nature of Sarah's argument is impressive. I was left with a worry that most of what I was to teach Sarah for the rest of the year would be unchallenging for her in that it was focussed on specific examples of physical phenomena and largely ignored the abstract principles which serve to draw these examples together. It seemed clear, however, that these principles were the things that really interested her.

As these anecdotes suggest, any assessment of differences amongst pupils, that we might make in order to plan teaching for specific pupils, will have to be based on detailed knowledge of the individual pupils themselves. However, in thinking more generally about ways of conceptualising our approach it can be helpful to look for some broad categories of difference. Having the range of categories in mind can be helpful in extending the scope of our investigations of a given pupil, and understanding the nature of each category can help us to avoid fundamentally inappropriate responses to a pupil.

In an earlier publication (McIntyre and Postlethwaite, 1989), we argued that there were several kinds of differences amongst pupils. We labelled these as:

- educational differences
- psychological differences
- physical differences
- social differences in classrooms
- socio-economic and cultural differences

and argued that, in relation to each, it was important to think about their relevance to the classroom, their stability, where the locus of control lies, how pervasive the differences are, and what value judgements are made about the differences. It is on these issues that the rest of this chapter is focused.

Figure 2.1 Sarah's argument about forces on currents in magnetic fields.

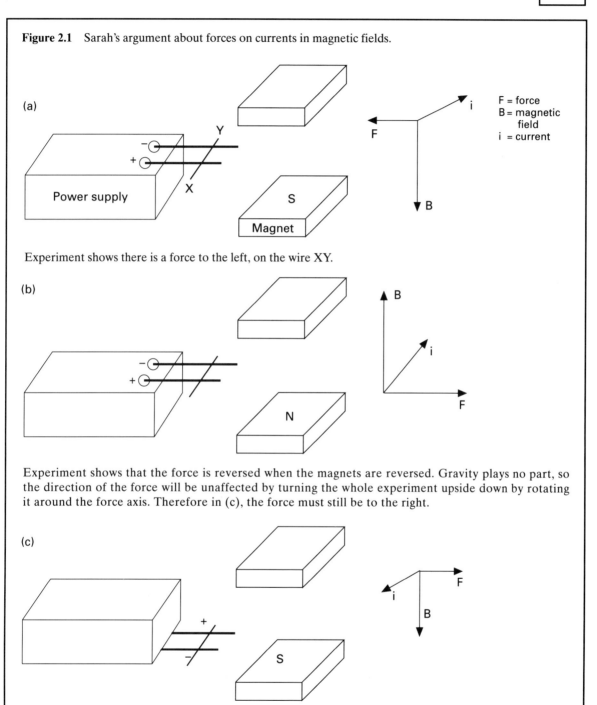

Experiment shows there is a force to the left, on the wire XY.

Experiment shows that the force is reversed when the magnets are reversed. Gravity plays no part, so the direction of the force will be unaffected by turning the whole experiment upside down by rotating it around the force axis. Therefore in (c), the force must still be to the right.

Note that rotating the power supply will place the positive terminal at the back. The set up is therefore just the same as (a), but with just the current reversed. Therefore, reversing the current alone must reverse the force.

EDUCATIONAL DIFFERENCES

Educational differences can be described as differences in what pupils already know, understand and can do in relation to the issue which is the subject of a planned education experience. The particular thing to note about educational differences is that they necessarily have a *direct* bearing on pupils' future learning. Since the very notion of learning implies modifying or extending what has already been learnt, differences in existing knowledge, understanding and skill must affect how readily and effectively a pupil can learn new material or new ways of doing things. Even rote learning of a spelling is impossible if that spelling is already known, or if letter names are not yet known. Meaningful learning of the concept of acceleration cannot be achieved without previous mastery, or concurrent teaching, of the concept of speed, and preferably that of velocity. Teaching about the role of density in explaining floating cannot be fully effective unless the pupil's personal explanation of why things float is understood, for only then can the teacher know what learning experiences might be appropriate either to support the child's view or to challenge it. This crucial point, that educational differences will affect learning, is not at all dependent on any particular theory of how learning takes place, but is simply a consequence of the meaning of the word 'learning' itself.

It may not be obvious *how* the teacher should take account of such things, but it is obvious that, to enable all pupils to learn as effectively as possible, the teacher must do so. This view is emphasised in Ausubel's (1968) much quoted remark: 'The most important single factor influencing learning is what the learner already knows.' It also forms the basis of Bloom's (1976) Theory of Mastery Learning which we discuss at length later in this book. There can therefore be no doubt that educational differences exist, and that they are highly relevant to the teacher's task. We would argue that this relevance arises directly out of the nature of education: it does not have to be demonstrated empirically.

Of course, much is already known of the variation in pupils' knowledge, understanding and skill in the area of science. Existing research findings from the Assessment of Performance Unit (APU), and from the wide range of studies of pupils' alternative frameworks can give some insights into the things pupils of a particular age are likely to know and be able to do, and into the things which are likely to cause them difficulties. The findings can also alert teachers to the range of likely differences amongst pupils.

We shall summarise some of these findings below. However, it is helpful first to draw attention to some of their limitations for our present purposes. In guiding a teacher's actions, nothing can substitute for direct investigation of the knowledge base of the individual pupils in a given class. This is particularly so if we are interested in individual children with special needs as their knowledge base might be expected to be varied and (like Lucy's) rather unexpected. There is also the point that the full range of pupils with special educational needs have rarely been the focus of the kinds of research mentioned above. For example, the APU survey specifically excluded pupils 'in special schools or in units designated as special within normal schools' (APU, 1982) from their enquiry, though by random sampling pupils in a representative sample of mainstream schools they clearly gained information about the largest part of the special needs group (the 'Warnock 18 per cent'). It is clear, therefore, that a teacher with concern for pupils with special educational needs would not want to rely exclusively on generalised research findings in planning how to respond to the whole range of individual differences amongst the pupils in their class. Nevertheless, such findings can serve as useful starting points for direct individual investigation on the part of the teacher.

Pupils' knowledge, understanding and skills

Children differ in what they know, understand and can do. One useful source of insights into these differences can be found in the series of reports from the APU (1989). In science, the assessment framework used to structure the APU survey covered the following areas (the labels for the APU categories are shown in parentheses):

- the assimilation of information presented in a variety of forms (1a)
- the communication, in various formats, of information and of the results of experiments (1b and c; 5c)
- the use of apparatus (2a, b and c) and observation (3a, b and c)
- the interpretation and application of scientific ideas, sometimes in circumstances where knowledge of taught science is not required (4a, b and c), sometimes where it is (4d and e)
- the design (5a, b and c) and performance (6) of investigations

This framework can be seen as consistent with views on the nature of science as a form of knowledge in which the experimental test for truth, and the characteristic ways of working, stand alongside the key concepts of the subject and the patterns of relationship amongst them in defining the nature of the subject area (Hirst and Peters, 1970). It does, however, emphasise the skills and techniques often referred to as the processes of science, rather than the concepts. The APU framework is also consistent with parts of current GCSE examination criteria (DES and Welsh Office, 1985a) and with elements of the formal definition of science in the National Curriculum (DES and Welsh Office, 1989b, 1991b), both of which it predates. However, it is not based on any particular theoretical model of pupils' learning in science.

The APU science reports can therefore be expected to give an interesting picture of the range of pupils' understanding of some parts of the content of science and, particularly, to show the kinds of strengths and weaknesses that pupils might display in carrying out the processes and skills of scientific investigation. This proves to be the case. For example, the report on 15-year olds (APU, 1988) shows that, in relation to Category 1, most pupils, including the least able, could identify the tallest person from a bar chart of heights of individuals, identify the food with the most protein from pie charts of the composition of different foods and indicate the time of day when the temperature was highest from a line graph. However, average and less-able 15-year olds had difficulty when graph interpretation required scale interpolation, when two or more quantities had to be manipulated arithmetically or when graphs were superimposed.

On many tasks involving the use of apparatus (Category 2): 'The lasting impression . . . is of positive achievement'. (APU, 1988, p. 52) However, APU also showed that, when readings from instruments involved interpolation, or when use of decimals to two places were required, many pupils had considerable difficulties in coming to correct answers. Furthermore, APU showed that boys were more competent than girls. We should, of course, be cautious of interpreting this as a difference in aptitude between the genders. The attitudes and expectations of adults regarding boys and girls, and the different opportunities they offer to them as youngsters, may be just as likely as explanations of the differences in attainment that the two groups show in use of apparatus.

In terms of making and interpreting observations (Category 3), only the most able were found to look beyond single observations even when the question cued them to do so. Less able pupils tended not to explain their observations, or to make explicit their interpretation of those observations. Interestingly, on this category, girls tended to perform better than boys.

In response to questions in Category 4, which required pupils to interpret presented information, less able pupils tended to score badly.

However, the report states (With original emphasis) (p. 74):

> . . . the failure of less able pupils to score may not be in some cases through innate incapacity to 'interpret' the information. Question-writing strategies which produce a greater involvement in the data, and which indicate *broadly* what kinds of methods and responses are indicated, can allow the deployment of competencies otherwise unused.

In this comment APU have gone beyond mapping pupil differences which the teacher might wish to take into account in planning teaching for all pupils, and have suggested ways in which he or she might structure support, during assessment and during normal teaching, for those who have the particular difficulty which has been identified. This is a useful example of the way in which the information summarised in this section might be used by teachers, and we shall return to ideas like this in later chapters.

As expected, the APU report also gives specific insights into pupils' understanding of some concepts. For example, in the context of questions on combustion, it appeared that only about half the pupils in the topmost of five, equal-sized performance groups (defined on the basis of pupils' total scores in APU test packages) had a clear enough grasp of the concepts to be able to elucidate quantitative aspects of the topic. Even though the questions did not require pupils to engage in actual calculations, all four remaining performance groups were similar in their inability to comment correctly on the quantitative outcomes of combustion. (For example, in all the lower four groups, the modal response to a question about phosphorus burning in a closed container of air was that there would be a mass decrease.) The report suggests that this profile of performance also applied to other concepts. Even the highest performing group seemed to experience difficulty in transferring their understanding of the concept of combustion to the (relatively) novel situation of the petrol engine.

Given the emphasis in recent science education on the teaching of concepts, it is perhaps surprising

that '. . . understanding of the concepts of taught science represents the area of lowest competence' (APU, 1988, p. 85). It is, perhaps, wise to note that the report warns of the difficulty of making valid generalisations about pupils' conceptual understanding on the basis of the kinds of tests used by APU. Nevertheless, APU's suggestions that this understanding could be improved by a '. . . reduced conceptual burden' and by '. . . diversity of illustration and application' (APU, 1988, p. 85) are helpful insights to which we shall return later.

In planning investigations (Category 5), pupils of all abilities tended to perform better on questions about handling variables than on questions about a range of operational details of an experiment. However, this difference was particularly marked for pupils in the bottom two performance groups. The questions on operational details required pupils to visualise an experimental activity describing how measurements might be taken, or what sequences of action might be needed, whereas the questions about specific variables were more clear cut. It is also interesting that, asked to identify variables that needed to be controlled, most pupils (including most of the least able pupils) could identify one variable. Able and less able pupils differed in their ability to identify more than one control variable. APU interpret this as showing that able pupils had a '. . . more sophisticated conceptual model of the situation.' However, questions about whether particular variables were relevant to an investigation or not seemed to be more uniformly answered across the whole range of pupil ability. Another finding in this category was that linguistic difficulties sometimes made it difficult to be sure that pupils extracted from questions the meaning that was intended by the question writers, and to be sure that markers were clear of the meanings which pupils intended in their answers. In some situations APU felt that interviews might be necessary if detailed maps of pupils' thinking were to be obtained.

The APU survey of pupils' ability to conduct practical investigations (Category 6) revealed that 'a very large majority' of pupils could work along logically sensible lines when investigating one dependent and one independent variable, and that just under half could deal with situations involving two independent variables. Control of variables was attempted, to some extent, by 'almost all pupils', though they were not always able to discuss the control steps which they had been observed to take and may have been simply 'keeping *everything* the same', rather than identifying *relevant* variables which needed to be controlled. To conduct an investigation, pupils needed to translate a general question such as 'Which is the best paper towel?' into a question about a variable that could be measured or observed. APU found that reformulation of the problem into one involving a quantitative measurement caused difficulty for many 15-year olds, that repetition of readings was undertaken by considerably less than half the pupils, with *systematic* repetition being a feature of less than 10 per cent of observed investigations, but that choice and use of apparatus was often appropriate. Generally more able pupils were observed to 'perform better in a fairly uniform manner across the aspects of tasks studied'. However, where tasks gave less able pupils opportunities to engage in simple concrete activities that closely matched the formal structure of a well-designed experiment (e.g. when they were offered springs of equal length but varying diameter, and springs of varying length and equal diameter, and were asked to investigate factors affecting how quickly a load bobs up and down) their ability to discuss that formal structure after carrying out the practical work was quite similar to that of more able pupils. Where manipulative complexity prevented less able pupils from engaging in practical exploration, their ability to discuss the formal structure of the experiment was less than that of their more able peers.

These brief comments on the findings of APU do nothing to map the richness of the surveys, but they do give some insight into the *kind* of information that can be acquired by reading the full range of reports that have been produced. Such information is clearly of considerable help to science teachers in indicating the kinds of variation that might be associated with ability differences in a class of a particular age, and the kinds

of work that could be expected to give difficulty for some groups of pupil. It can clearly provide clues to how the teacher might then respond. However, it is helpful to repeat the point made at the beginning of this section: namely that general information of this kind can never replace the need for individual investigation of pupils' attainments, especially where pupils with special educational needs are concerned. It is also important to remember that the APU findings relate to the particular context of science education that existed at the time the surveys were carried out around the beginning of the 1980s. That context has changed considerably in the meantime and pupils patterns of attainment may well have changed as a result.

Pupils' alternative frameworks

In science in particular, the notion of pupils' alternative frameworks has become another important source of insight into possible educational differences amongst pupils. The idea of alternative frameworks does have a strong theoretical base which lies in the Personal Construct Psychology of Kelly (1955). The frameworks arise as pupils strive to construct their own meaning for, and understanding of, the experiences that they have. These personal, perhaps idiosyncratic, frameworks are then used by pupils to explain and predict phenomena that they encounter. The frameworks, which may not be at all similar to accepted scientific explanations, do nevertheless work for the pupil who has constructed them. At least, they work in the, perhaps limited, range of circumstances in which the pupil usually operates. These personally constructed frameworks interact with more widely accepted 'scientific' explanations offered by teachers, and can affect how the pupil responds to the things that the teacher says. Since the alternative frameworks usually serve the pupil concerned quite well, they may not readily be displaced by the teacher's explanations, especially as these are often more complex. The pupil's personal framework may be particularly resistant to change because it generally provides more or less successful predictions within the context that the pupil normally operates, whereas to appreciate the greater range of application of the teacher's explanation, the pupil has to consider situations which s/he does not normally encounter. The greater power of the formal explanation may therefore be seen as a small advantage which is greatly outweighed by the increased difficulty of the ideas.

Various summaries and discussions of work in this field exist (e.g. Driver, 1983; Gilbert and Watts, 1983; Osborne and Freyberg, 1985). Interestingly, some of the investigations of alternative frameworks have been based on data derived from the APU surveys we have discussed above. These data have been re-analysed, and sometimes extended by use of additional questions focussed more specifically on the alternative frameworks issue. Other investigations have been based on completely independent data, sometimes collected by interview with pupils, rather than tests as such.

We cannot hope to give a comprehensive view of the results of this work here. Nevertheless, it might be helpful to indicate something of the nature of pupils' alternative frameworks by reference to one or two examples. For instance, Osborne and Freyberg have reported that, in answer to a multiple-choice format question about a candle burning in daylight, some 60 per cent of a sample of 144 12-year olds who had not studied light in any formal way stated that the light stayed on the candle, whereas about 20 per cent stated that the light came out until it hit something. In response to a similar question about a candle burning in the dark, about 10 per cent of the 12-year olds thought that light stayed on the candle, and nearly 50 per cent felt that it came out until it hit something. While the proportion of correct answers to both questions was greater for a sample of 235 13-year olds who had studied light, the misconception that light stayed on the candle during the day was persistent: just over 40 per cent of pupils continued to give this answer. Similar multiple-choice questions revealed that less than 40 per cent of a sample of 17-year olds thought that bubbles in boiling water contained steam; about 35 per cent thought they were hydrogen or

oxygen, about 20 per cent thought they were air and a few pupils thought they were 'heat'. Osborne and Freyberg go on to discuss pupils' views of the concepts 'living', 'plant' and 'animal', and their ideas about electric current, force, motion under gravity, evaporation and burning. (They also provide a table of over 80 references to papers giving a fuller picture of the work that has been done, mainly in the area of the physical sciences.)

Similar examples can be found in the collection of papers edited by Archenhold et al. (1980) and in Driver et al. (1985). Of course, as in the case of the APU results, we might expect that pupils who experience a different science curriculum at school will acquire different alternative explanations for phenomena, for one influence on children's thinking is likely to be the formal science teaching which they receive. We might tentatively predict that children in the UK will soon have rather different alternative frameworks from those which are currently reported in the literature because of the increased significance of science in the primary school curriculum following the introduction of the National Curriculum. However, Driver et al. (1985) offers some interesting general comments about such frameworks which may well represent a more fundamental insight into children's thinking, and which may hold true across a range of science teaching contexts. These general comments may be particularly helpful in guiding teachers' exploration of individual pupils' concepts and in planning responses to them. Driver and her colleagues reported that:

- children tend to be dominated by the perceptual features of a situation rather than to emphasise underlying concepts (thus sugar disappears in water, rather than continuing to exist as dispersed particles too small to see)
- they tend to focus on one aspect of a situation rather than on all relevant changes (cf. Piaget's notion of centring)
- they tend to concentrate on characteristics of situations which change rather than on aspects which remain fixed, and may fail to apply ideas derived in changing situations to steady state ones (e.g. forces may be recognised in

connection with motion but be ignored in statics problems)

- they tend to think in terms of linear change and may find it difficult to think of two-way or multi-way interactions (e.g. energy input to cause melting is much more readily accepted than energy release during freezing; reversible chemical change and equilibrium are more difficult to understand than one-way processes)
- they tend to use a single concept which includes elements from a range of scientific concepts and to use it in a rather undifferentiated way (e.g. electrical power is used with a meaning which includes parts of the concepts of current, charge and potential difference)
- they sometimes use different ideas to explain essentially the same phenomenon if that phenomenon is presented in rather different contexts, but they also have some favourite ideas which influence the nature of their thinking in a range of situations

It is easy to see that this kind of insight into the general nature of children's thinking, and into the kind of differences that might exist in the frameworks used by different individuals in connection with scientific phenomena, could be of enormous benefit to the science teacher if appropriate ways of responding to them could be developed. For our present purposes the two most important points which emerge from this field are first that there *are* insights available into pupils' alternative frameworks, and secondly that these frameworks will necessarily affect pupils' learning as, once formed, they can be quite resistant to change.

PSYCHOLOGICAL DIFFERENCES

Another important category of variation amongst pupils is that of psychological differences. This includes quantitative differences amongst pupils in such general cognitive characteristics as intelligence, and in specific abilities such as spatial or mathematical abilities, as well as qualitative differences amongst them in such areas as their feelings about a subject and about themselves as learners of that subject, their Piagetian stage of development, their preferred cognitive styles, and the ways in which they seek to explain their own successes and failures.

It is probably true to say that all psychological characteristics which are subject to quantitative measurement are held by different people to different degrees. Indeed, characteristics which showed no variation would have no predictive power and would therefore be of only limited interest. It is this question of predictive power that makes psychological differences interesting to educationalists. If variation on a given characteristic can be shown to be related to pupils' different levels of success in learning in the school environment, then teachers might find knowledge of pupils' scores on that characteristic of value in planning their teaching. The crucial point here is that any relationship between the characteristic and the pupils' learning has to be established empirically: there is no logically inescapable reason to prevent a pupil with low IQ, say, from learning any skill or concept if an appropriate way of teaching that skill or concept to that pupil is devised. If experiment does show a link between IQ and learning, then we might be wise to take account of IQ in our educational planning, but in doing so we should bear in mind that the link can only be assumed to hold in the circumstances in which the experiment was done. It is perfectly logical to look for different ways of teaching that might break that link. An unfavourable score on any psychological characteristic may therefore alert us to the need to deal with a pupil in a different way, but it is not a trap which condemns that pupil to poor levels of performance whatever we, as teachers, do to help.

Given this view of psychological differences, it may be helpful to discuss some examples and to indicate something of what is known of their links to educational outcomes. We will begin with several kinds of difference in which people hold given attributes to varying degrees; we will then consider other 'qualitative' psychological differences where it is the nature of the attribute itself which varies from person to person; finally we will consider some differences derived from information processing models.

General intelligence

An important psychological characteristic is that of general intelligence. This concept relates to the commonsense observation that some people are generally more 'intelligent' than others, in the sense that they engage in behaviour, across a wide range of activities, which tends to be effective in solving problems and leading them to the goals which they desire. More formally, the concept of general intelligence rests on the positive correlations that exist between an individual's results on a range of tests, each of which is designed to cover one of several problem types. General intelligence can therefore be identified with the general factor which can be derived from results on that range of tests through the statistical procedure known as *factor analysis* (Child, 1981). Sometimes a set of factors, rather than a single general factor, can be generated by factor analysis of test results, but where these are non-orthogonal, they can themselves be subjected to factor analysis, often resulting in a second order factor which can then be interpreted as general intelligence (Sternberg, 1985). General intelligence can therefore be taken as nothing more than an empirical construct summarising test correlations. It can, however, be seen as a consequence of the notion that certain components of intelligence (particularly some of those metacomponents such as planning, monitoring and evaluating, which serve an executive function in intelligent behaviour) come into play in a very wide range of tasks and therefore encourage a common performance level for an individual on all such tasks (Sternberg, 1985).

IQ tests, which provide measures of general intelligence, certainly reveal differences in this characteristic amongst people. Indeed, the fact that they are constructed so that they have a given standard deviation implies that differences between people are central to the very notion of the IQ test. The empirical evidence for the educational significance of general intelligence comes mainly from studies which reveal the power of IQ in predicting pupils' later performance on educationally important tasks. For example, Zigler and Seitz (1982) state that (p. 598),

> Despite the many shortcomings of an IQ score, no other measure has been found to be related to so many other behaviours of theoretical and practical significance.

They go on to quote correlations of 0.70 between IQ and school performance, without indicating exactly what aspects of school performance they were reporting on. Vernon (1957) does, however, give quite specific correlations between IQ and School Certificate results: 0.51 (mathematics); 0.50 (English); 0.39 (chemistry). These figures clearly suggest that IQ has relevance to learning in schools.

The existence of this link between IQ and performance in school *is* important. It is, however, equally important to note several other things about it:

- even a correlation of 0.70 leaves just over 50 per cent of the variance in the respective area of school work unaccounted for, so IQ does matter, but so do other things unrelated to IQ

- in some subject areas the correlation is not as big as those quoted above (biology: IQ = 0.12; art: IQ = – 0.02; Vernon, 1957)
- although correlations between IQ and school performance are often high, correlations between IQ and 'everyday performance in life in the postschool period' are small – perhaps about 0.20 (McClelland, 1973)
- IQ itself is not a fixed characteristic for individual pupils: it can be altered through training programmes such as Instrumental Enrichment (Feuerstein, 1980)
- even where large correlations do exist they can only be assumed to apply in the teaching and learning situations that were experienced by the pupils who were studied; in other situations the links could be much weaker
- correlations should not be taken to imply causative links; IQ and achievement may be correlated, but high or low IQ may not be the cause of high or low performance in school

These points reinforce, for IQ, the general statement which was made about psychological differences above: an unfavourable score on an IQ test may alert us to the need to deal with a pupil in a different way, but it is not a trap which condemns that pupil to poor levels of performance whatever we, as teachers, may do to help.

Specific abilities

We indicated above that general intelligence can be related to the common variance of scores from a range of tests. However, some psychologists place much more importance on those elements of the variance in test scores which are not common and consequently derive models of intelligence in which several specific abilities play a significant, and sometimes dominant, part. An early version of this approach was that of Thurstone which resulted in a model consisting of nine 'Primary Mental Abilities', such as Verbal Comprehension, Number Facility and Perceptual Speed (Thurstone, 1938). A highly elaborate version exists in the 'Structure of Intellect' (SI) Model developed by Guilford (1959, 1967) in which 120 different specific abilities were postulated and the notion of general ability was rejected. Guilford has subsequently updated the model: he now predicts 150 abilities and claims to have demonstrated the existence of 105 of them (Guilford, 1977, 1982). Some argue that Guilford's model is little more than a statistical artifact (Eysenck, 1967), but there does seem to be some acceptance of the idea of specific abilities, even if their exact structure is still a matter for debate.

Given such models, it is not surprising that a test of any specific component of intelligence reveals individual variation on that component, and that sets of tests covering a range of components reveal different profiles of scores for different pupils. The educational significance of these profiles has, of course, to be established empirically.

Guilford has shown that some 20 abilities within his SI Model are closely related to school performance, and that, where individual pupils have strengths on some SI abilities, these can be used to help them to raise their performance on other abilities within the model on which they showed weaknesses. This clearly has potential for the teacher seeking ways to help pupils improve performance across the range of demands placed upon them in school.

The educational significance of other ways of charting specific abilities have also been explored. For example, some specific abilities can be measured by the Differential Aptitude Test (DAT) battery which provides score on sub-tests such as Verbal Reasoning, Space Relations, Mechanical Reasoning, and Language Usage (Bennett et al., 1974). Denton and Postlethwaite (1985) investigated the relationship between 13-year old pupils' scores on these DAT sub-tests and performance of those same pupils at age 16 in public examinations in four subject areas. The pupils' scores on the DAT sub-tests were related to subsequent O-level scores in English, French, physics and mathematics through the process of stepwise multiple regression. In each subject area the statistical procedure generated a 'prediction equation' consisting of the weighted combination of DAT results that was found to be the best predictor for the O-level score in that subject. Different sub-tests were found to feature in each of the four prediction equations indicating that different DAT profiles were related to high performance in these four subjects. Interestingly, in each subject, the weighted combination of appropriate DAT scores provided a better prediction of O-level score than did IQ alone.

Individual sub-tests of the DAT battery have been shown to be predictive of post-school performance in specific tasks. Otherwise, all the points made in relation to the educational significance of IQ continue to apply in relation to specific abilities.

Personality, motivation and attitudes

Although some theories of personality emphasise the individualistic nature of personality attributes (see, for example, the psychoanalytic theories of the Freudian school), others (e.g. Eysenck, 1953; Cattell, 1965, 1970) are concerned with placing individuals at an appropriate point along a pre-determined dimension or trait. Using a factor analytical approach similar to that used to develop multidimensional models of intelligence, Eysenck identified two main personality dimensions: 'extroversion–introversion' which relates to how socially outgoing a person is, and 'neuroticism–stability' which relates to a person's tendency to be anxious. Similar methodology led Cattell to propose a model with 16 personality factors but these were intercorrelated. Two of the main categories into which Cattell's factors can be grouped were concerned with extroversion and anxiety. Therefore, in terms of the dimensions of personality, the differences between Cattell's and Eysenck's models are not very great (Cohen and Manion, 1981).

The relationship between school performance and personality traits of these kinds are not straightforward, but they have been shown to exist. Cohen and Manion (1981) point out that the link between 'extroversion–introversion' and performance is age related. Below the age of about 14, extroverts performed better than introverts;

above about 14, the relationship was reversed. Evidence for a link between the dimension of 'neuroticism–stability' and performance is less clear cut but can be inferred from experiments which have shown that performance within a given teaching style can depend on pupils' levels of anxiety: Seiber et al. (1977) showed that in a teaching style that placed considerable reliance on students' memories, anxious pupils did less well than those who showed lower levels of anxiety. It is interesting that in teaching styles imposing lower memory loads the differences in performance between students of different levels of anxiety were not in evidence. This is a nice example of our assertion that evidence for a link between a psychological characteristic and school performance in one context should not be regarded as evidence for an inevitable link in all contexts.

Clearly, then, personality differences can have effects on educational attainment, though the precise nature of those effects is complex. Clearly, too, teachers can act in ways which will reduce the disadvantage which appears to be suffered by pupils with some personality traits.

Closely related to the personality traits discussed above are aspects of motivation. The motives underlying human activity have been very differently conceived in different theories. Weiner (1985) divides such theories into three broad groups. The first of these comprises psychoanalytic and drive theories which argue that actions are taken to reduce tension or satisfy needs. Weiner states that such models place relatively little weight on any cognitive processes that might be involved in stimulating behaviour. Weiner's second group includes theories such as Atkinson's Theory of Achievement Motivation which, he argues, have a much greater cognitive content in that they assume that humans are motivated by the value they place on certain goals and the expectations they have that given behaviour will lead towards those goals. Weiner's third group includes personal construct theory, attribution theory and the humanistic theories of Maslow and Rogers which explain motivation in terms of people's striving for understanding of themselves and their environment, and for what Maslow describes as self-actualisation (i.e. striving for self awareness, self acceptance, spontaneity, creativity, etc.).

The place of individual differences in motivational theory is complex. Weiner (1985) reports, for example, that psychologists pursuing psychoanalytic and drive theories paid much less attention to individual differences than did Atkinson for whom such differences were highly significant.

Where individual differences have been regarded as psychologically important (e.g. in connection with the concept of 'need for achievement' (nAch)) it is important to ask if they have any educational significance. This has been investigated, but the results prove to be somewhat complex. Links between nAch scores and educational performance have certainly been found (McClelland, 1955; Raynor, 1970), but sometimes links between nAch and achievement have not appeared in experiments designed to detect them. Lavin (1965) provides a useful review of some of these studies. One possible reason for the conflicting results is that achievement is affected by so many factors that great variation can be expected amongst people with similar nAch scores (Weiner, 1985). Another is that the profile of students' nAch and anxiety scores taken together may offer a better predictor of achievement than either of these characteristics taken separately (Cronbach and Snow, 1977).

Need for achievement, particularly in association with anxiety, may therefore be an educationally relevant psychological difference. It is, however important to note that most of the detailed work on nAch is based on male subjects, and that where females are studied, data appear to show less systematic relationships. This serves only to reinforce our major conclusion that links between motivation and educational performance are unusually complex. This can also be confirmed by reference to literature on the educational implications of other motivational dimensions such as 'need for affiliation' (Cronbach and Snow, 1977).

In Chapter 3, I will outline some possible tactics for the teacher who is trying to respond to individual differences in motivation amongst pupils and will draw on the different theoretical models of motivation in doing so. At this point it is perhaps worth stressing that the established complexity of the field raises doubts about simplistic ideas for teaching methods that may support less motivated pupils (e.g. by simply making the material or lesson more interesting or, in a general sense, more relevant to adult life), and suggests that, although these may be necessary elements in a teacher's response they will not, alone, enable us to respond fully to pupils to this kind.

The preceding discussion has been linked to the various psychological models of personality and motivation. A brief, and more pragmatic discussion of studies which have demonstrated the educational significance of individual differences in pupils' attitudes will now be given. I shall mention attitudes to a specific subject, to school in general and attitudes towards self as a learner.

Pupils' attitudes towards a subject can be assessed by questionnaire asking such things as how much they would like to continue with study of that subject, and what they like or dislike about it. Such attitude scores have been correlated with achievement in the same subject, typical results being correlations of the order of 0.3–0.4 (Bloom, 1976). Such results imply that these attitudinal scores can account for 10–20 per cent of the variance in achievement. In the specific context of science, Ormerod and Duckworth (1975) have produced a detailed review of research on pupils' attitudes and leave their reader in no doubt about the educational relevance of pupils' attitudes to the subject.

Bloom (1976) also reported that correlations of the order of 0.3–0.4 were found between pupils' general attitude to school and their academic achievements. Of course it is possible that attitudes to school could be influenced by ability factors which themselves relate (as we have seen) to performance. One could, for example, speculate on a mechanism in which high ability leads to early success in school which in turn generates high levels of later performance and favourable attitudes. It is therefore particularly interesting to find that attitude scores have been found to have predictive validity for academic achievement over and above any that might be accounted for through such links. Denton and Postlethwaite (1985) related pupil characteristics at 13 to subsequent performance in O-level examinations at 16. The measures of specific cognitive abilities provided by the Differential Aptitude Test battery were part of the set of 13-year olds' characteristics that were used in this study and their links to examination performance have already been discussed. However, a set of attitude scales, originally developed for primary school children by Barker-Lunn (1970), and later modified by Ferri (1971) for secondary age pupils, were also included. These were found to enter in to some of the multiple regression equations linking 13-year-old characteristics and 16-year-old performance. For example, the attitude 'Relationship with Teacher' was found to enter in to the equation predicting performance in O-level English, after the DAT scales 'Language Usage', 'Spelling' and 'Verbal Reasoning'. The significance of this finding for the present discussion is that the statistical procedure that was used would only have drawn this attitude scale into the equation, in fourth place, if the attitude contributed additional predictive power, *over and above any that might have been present because of correlations between it and the DAT scales already entered*. This can be interpreted as clear evidence that attitudinal variations on the part of pupils can, in their own right, be important to the teacher if he or she is to help all pupils to learn effectively.

Finally, it is interesting to ask about the educational value of individual differences in pupils' academic self-image. Bloom (1976) quotes several studies in which this has been investigated by correlating self-image scores with academic achievement. The median correlation across all studies considered for pupils in the early secondary age range was 0.49 indicating a link which should be taken seriously. There is other interesting evidence that suggests that there is a relationship, particularly for boys, between low academic self-image scores and disruptive behaviour (Gray and Richer, 1988). Behavioural outcomes are important in their own right, so irrespective of links with academic performance, there would seem

to be good reason for teachers to consider this aspect of individual pupil variation.

Qualitative psychological differences

Bannister and Fransella (1980) criticise much of the study of individual differences of personality, as (p. 47)

> . . . the study of group samenesses. Here we have focussed on the establishment of general dimensions, at some point along which all individuals can be placed, rather than on the study of the dimensions which each individual develops in order to organise their own world.

This criticism could be taken to apply to many of the other aspects of difference discussed so far in this chapter. To redress the balance, I shall now turn to some of the qualitative ways in which pupils differ. The issue here is not, 'Where does Jane lie on some *predetermined* dimension of personality, or understanding?', but 'In what ways do the particular characteristics of Jane's personality or understanding differ, qualitatively, from those of other people?'.

One good example of the particular structures which individuals develop to make sense of their own world is that of the alternative frameworks which pupils build to explain phenomena to themselves. We have already discussed these and argued that they should be classified as educational, rather than psychological differences, since they have direct bearing on pupils' subsequent learning. However, according to Kelly's (1955) Personal Construct Theory, pupils actively construct their own understanding of more general aspects of their world: they not only build their own models of why things float or of what is meant by political power, they also construct their own ways of thinking about friends, or teachers, or school subjects or school generally. For example, one pupil may set up a system of dimensions (constructs) to help them understand their friends in which these friends are each placed on the dimensions of 'is fun–is boring' and 'conforms–rebels'; another pupil may seek to understand the same set of friends in terms of the single dimension 'selfish–helps others'. These two pupils do not simply disagree in quantitative terms on where a given friend lies on the dimension of conformity. Their disagreement is more fundamental; the difference between them is qualitative. One does not use the dimension of conformity at all in seeking to understand their friends' behaviour and attitudes. It would seem likely that knowledge of the differences between these two individual construct systems would be important for a teacher who wants to understand the dynamics of the peer group so as to devise activities to encourage that group to work together in ways that will maximise the learning of all the pupils involved.

Similarly, pupils' constructs of their teachers, of school subjects, or of school generally can be expected to differ, as each construct system is created by each individual in an attempt to make sense of their whole range of relevant experience. These more general constructs, and the individual differences associated with them, might sensibly be classified as psychological differences. As such, we would argue that their relevance for education needs to be demonstrated empirically. Unfortunately, though several studies of *teachers'* constructs of pupils exist (e.g. Wood and Napthali, 1975; Postlethwaite, 1984; Postlethwaite and Jaspars, 1986) studies of *pupils'* constructs, and especially studies of the educational significance of such constructs, seem to be rare. The *British Education Index*, for example, catalogues 24 publications dealing with personal construct psychology in the period 1978–88, but only three of these are centrally concerned with pupils' or students' own constructs and even these tend not to be focussed on the educational significance of those constructs.

Another interesting area in which qualitative differences may exist amongst pupils is concerned with how individuals explain their own success or failure at tasks. This work, which is described as Attribution Theory (see, for example, Kelley, 1972), suggests that people explain their own success and failure in terms of causes such as ability, luck, ease or difficulty of the task, and amount of effort devoted to the task. The kinds of attributions

made depend on such things as the success of others on the task (if many fail, an individual who fails is more likely to produce attributions based on task difficulty than those based on low personal ability), and the person's own record of past success (if a pupil usually succeeds but fails on a given task, the explanation of that failure is more likely to be in terms of luck or effort than ability). There is a suggestion that attributions have an ego-protective element: success is likely to be attributed to personal characteristics, failure to factors outside the individual's control.

Attempts to systematise the attributions produced by individuals have led to a three-dimensional model in which individual attributions are classified as either stable or unstable, internal or external, and controllable or uncontrollable (Weiner, 1985). As in the case of personal constructs, attributions are generated by individuals to make sense of their range of relevant experiences and of the circumstances in which these occurred. Individual differences in attribution are therefore inevitable. Some group differences have also been suggested (e.g. that boys are more likely to make external attributions of failure whereas girls are likely to attribute failure to internal causes).

It is also clear that the attributions pupils make may influence their subsequent performance. Raviv et al. (1980) has shown that advantaged pupils tended to attribute success to internal stable causes such as high ability. Continued success was therefore expected. They tended to attribute failure to internal but unstable causes such as the amount of effort put in to the task. Since this implies that future success lies within their own sphere of control (they can choose to put in more effort next time), such pupils were inclined to persist with efforts to succeed. Disadvantaged pupils tended to attribute failure to internal stable causes such as low ability and therefore expected to fail again. In such circumstances there is no logical reason why they should make any further effort. Thus pupils' attributions matter to teachers in two senses: the teachers can affect attributions that are made by the circumstances they create in their classrooms, and these attributions can affect pupils' later engagement in the tasks the teachers set.

Other examples of qualitative differences amongst pupils lie in areas of cognitive development and cognitive style. Piaget's work on the development of thinking is well known. In his model, children pass through stages of cognitive development in the following order: the sensorimotor stage; the pre-operational stage (sub-divided into the pre-conceptual and the intuitive); the concrete operational stage (sometimes sub-divided into early and late concrete operations); the formal operational stage (again sometimes subdivided into early and late stages). A teacher can gain a view of the stage at which pupils are functioning from the responses they make in the work they are doing. One could argue that a teacher can modify teaching to take account of these responses without the additional baggage of Piagetian theory. Doubtless there is some truth in this, but an advantage of the theory is that one can (with the caution that should always attend extrapolation) make assumptions about other aspects of a pupil's thinking once observation has enabled one to place that pupil at a particular stage.

Piaget assigned ages to the different stages, but children do not pass cleanly from one stage to another. Instead they tend to move backwards and forwards between adjacent stages, only gradually becoming more consistent in the more sophisticated thinking of the higher stage (Cohen, 1983), and even when confident in formal operations, the child may still continue to function in many day to day situations at a concrete level (Child, 1981). Also, the rate at which individual children pass through the stages varies considerably: Shayer and Adey (1981) suggest that at the age of 11 about 7 per cent of pupils will not yet be at the stage of early concrete operations, whereas at 14 years some 7 per cent will have reached the late formal stage. Thus a teacher concerned with pupils who have special educational needs, and with able pupils, may find it helpful to have an understanding of the characteristics of all Piaget's stages (except perhaps the sensori-motor stage).

In Piaget's model, pupils at the *pre-conceptual* stage can be thought of as dominated by particular instances. The child is dominated by their own particular point of view and does not recognise that a given scene, looked at from a different direction, would look different. General concepts are not used, and if two particular instances are seen to go together on one occasion, they are assumed to go together on all occasions. At the *intuitive* stage, the child tends to concentrate on one aspect of a situation rather than looking at all aspects. This 'centring' gives rise to the well-known conservation problems where a child watching one of two equal balls of plasticine being rolled out will say that the rolled one is now bigger – because it has got longer. The judgement is an intuitive one based on an assessment on one aspect, rather than a carefully reasoned one based on all aspects. At this stage the child is not capable of mentally reversing a procedure (which also contributes to the error over the plasticine, for once you see that the rolled out ball can be rolled up again you can begin to argue that there must have been no change in the amount of material). At the stage of *concrete operations*, pupils can see both similarities and differences in a set of things and can put objects into order (e.g. in order of size), so meaningful classification of things becomes possible. At this stage conservation problems begin to sort themselves out, but pupils are still dominated by the particular situation confronting them at the moment and cannot see the range of other possibilities that could exist. It is at the stage of *formal operations* that pupils can finally work with the whole gamut of logical thought, able to distinguish reality and hypothesis and to pay proper attention to both. The distinction between pupils at the stages of concrete operations and formal operations can, perhaps, be summed up crudely but effectively in the following example. A red-headed girl is asked to consider the syllogism:

All red-heads are boys
I am a red-head
Therefore I am a boy.

If she is at the stage of concrete operations, the girl is likely to reply that the logic of the statements is faulty because she is a red-head and she is a girl. If she is at the stage of formal operations, the girl is able to see past the concrete example of her own hair colour and sex to the soundness of the syllogism as a piece of formal thinking.

The qualitative difference in thinking implied by these stages, and the associated development of pupils' abilities to appreciate such things as conservation of number, volume and mass, are still the subject of debate amongst psychologists (see, for example, Donaldson, 1978; Mogdil and Mogdil, 1982), but in so far as it is possible to assign a given pupil to a given stage, it is clearly helpful for the teacher to take account of the characteristics of thought at that stage if the pupil is to be taught effectively. There are various suggestions to guide teachers' attempts to match teaching to pupils' Piagetian stage. These include a detailed set of suggestions from Shayer and Adey (1981) which are directly concerned with the teaching of science. An alternative approach is to attempt to accelerate pupils' progress through the earlier stages. I shall return very briefly to this notion in Chapter 3.

The issue of *cognitive style* is also about the ways in which people think, though the focus is different from that of Piaget. Rather than conceptualising differences in terms of stages through which individuals pass, cognitive style theorists (like some of the investigators of personality to whom we have already referred) have tended to set up several bipolar dimensions along which each person can be placed in terms of the way in which they prefer to tackle problems. These dimensions include field dependence–field independence, focussing–scanning, and reflectivity–impulsivity (Fontana, 1977) and holist–serialist (Pask, 1975).

Compared with the field-independent person, the field-dependent person prefers to take a more global view of what is perceived, may find it difficult to pick out an element from its surroundings, and may have trouble remembering the details of something with which he or she has been presented. Cronbach and Snow (1977) present some evidence for the educational significance of field dependence. They report a study which indicated that field-independent boys performed best in a didactic teaching style whereas field-dependent boys did best in a discovery-based style. This is consistent with the notion that field-dependent people take a more global view of a situation.

People who are 'focusers' tend to delay forming a hypothesis about something until they have assembled enough evidence to make that hypothesis quite a likely one; scanners prefer to jump in with a hypothesis, hold on to it in the face of further evidence and have to go back and start again if their original idea is shown to be no longer tenable. As Fontana (1977) points out, these differences will matter in the classroom as scanners need the chance to review earlier information if they find their original idea was wrong, and focusers may find the pace of the classroom too high to allow them to formulate their ideas in the first place.

Reflective children tend to be slow as they weigh up alternative answers and are able to tolerate long periods of indecision while this process is worked through, impulsive children respond quickly, but not necessarily correctly. Again there would seem to be implications for the fast moving work of the classroom.

Holists prefer to concern themselves with the whole area under consideration, and to look for interconnections and analogies amongst the various parts, whereas serialists tend to follow the logical connections within one aspect of the topic to the initial exclusion of other elements of the topic. Just as holists may fail to examine and learn from the logical structure of subsections of a topic, so serialists may fail to benefit from what might be helpful analogies and tend not to form an overall vision of the work and its relationships to other things. Pask (1975) describes a study in which he has shown that these learning styles relate to learning outcomes. In particular he has shown that people learn more effectively when they are taught in a style which matches their preferred learning style.

Insights from information processing models

Information processing models offer us a picture of how people think. They are concerned with such things as:

- the ways in which we attend, selectively, to sensory input and store it in memory
- the ways in which information in memory is retrieved and processed
- the ways in which processing is internally supervised
- the ways in which results are output in the various overt and covert modes that enable us to influence our environment

Different researchers have somewhat different notions of the details of these elements of information processing (see for example, Sternberg, 1988) and there is still much to be understood about the ways in which the elements are combined into, for example, the inductive, deductive, or creative problem solving strategies which are elements of intelligent activity. In our present context, a particularly interesting notion is that individuals may differ qualitatively in the combinations of processes which they use for, and therefore the nature of the strategies that they bring to bear on, given problems (Sternberg, 1988).

Studies related to information processing models have already revealed many characteristics of children with learning problems which could be most helpful in guiding teachers in ways of helping such children to learn more effectively. I will summarise some of these characteristics below. Many of them relate to the internal self-supervision, or monitoring, of problem solving behaviour. This is a particularly interesting area, as monitoring is an aspect of thinking which is common to all kinds of problem solving whichever other information processing elements are being employed. The monitoring process may therefore generate the common element which can be found across the range of aspects of a pupil's performance, and which gets measured as 'general intelligence'.

Borkowski et al. (1984) and Ashman (1984) report that a common finding in research on memory and problem solving is that pupils with learning difficulties sometimes have appropriate strategies to solve a problem – that they can do all the necessary component steps – but that they do not spontaneously bring these strategies

into play, and do not coordinate the sequence of steps to take them through to a solution of the problem.

Sternberg (1984) quotes extensive evidence for the idea that pupils with learning difficulties do not monitor their own problem solving in effective ways. They do not keep track of where they are in the problem, do not allocate time appropriately (e.g. to planning and execution of a problem-solving approach), and do not recognise strategies which are taking them up dead ends. In some studies it has been shown that pupils will persist with a strategy even after they have been shown that it can take them nowhere, and have even altered the problem so that, in their own new terms, their flawed strategy works.

Sternberg also argues that such pupils tend not to be able to identify exactly what the problem is that they are being asked to tackle. This may be closely related to findings from other researchers (see Ashman, 1984) which have indicated that pupils with learning difficulties tend to perform less well when novel cues were embedded in the tasks they had to tackle and when they had to distinguish between relevant and irrelevant information.

Poor ability to attend to the task in hand is another characteristic of children with learning problems (Lupart and Mulcahy, 1984). A cognitive view of such shortcomings in attention is that they result from background knowledge which is insufficient, and cognitive strategies which are not sufficiently developed, to allow the pupil to focus on the task in hand. Lack of attention is therefore closely related to the inability to distinguish between relevant and irrelevant information, and is influenced by the familiarity of the task and the level of motivation which the pupil has for completing it. On this model there is a qualitative difference in the thinking of a pupil who is attending and one who is not and, since lack of attention is seen as a matter of knowledge and cognitive ability, rather than simply as a matter of will, there is clearly potential for helping pupils to be more effective in attending.

Children with learning difficulties have been shown to be less effective than their more able peers at remembering things. This may to some extent be a structural problem, but it also appears to be related to the way in which children use their memories (Campione et al., 1982; Ashman, 1984). Ashman, for example, describes children with IQ around 70 as:

- less effective at rehearsing on input (i.e. of going over in their mind the earlier elements of a list of points to be remembered while receiving the later items)
- less inclined to chunk things together on input (e.g. would remember 1,9,2,7 as four separate numbers rather than chunking them together into a four-figure number, or a pair of two-figure numbers)
- less able to use classifications to help to cluster items when recalling them (e.g. one may recall a long list more effectively if one remembers that there are six animals and two trees in the list – the classification enable one to search for clusters of items)
- less able to make use of redundancy in material to reduce memory load (e.g. would remember 3,4,5,3,4,5,3,4,5,3,4,5 as 12 separate digits rather than four lots of 3,4,5)

Not surprising, pupils with learning difficulties have been found to be slower than other children, not only on large scale school tasks but also on quite specific cognitive functions (Sperber and McCauley, 1984). They tend to be imprecise, impulsive and non-systematic in gathering information, either from real-world observation or from books (see relevant evidence presented by Ross and Ross, 1981). They have difficulty with 'if–then' links (Byrnes and Spitz, 1977) and they find it difficult to generalise from one situation to another (see a sequence of chapters on this topic in Brooks, 1984). They also have a poorer knowledge base than other children, both as a consequence of the characteristics described above, and perhaps as a cause of at least some of them.

A common reaction to this list of characteristics is that they seem to describe most pupils! It is probably true that most people display some of them to some extent, some of the time. The distinguishing feature of pupils with learning problems may be the depth, extent and consistency of these characteristics in their problem solving. However, the similarity with other pupils does tend to reinforce the view that there is nothing special about teaching pupils with special needs. That good teaching for them is simply good teaching. That in turn reinforces our view that proper attention to the needs of such pupils cannot be divorced from the issue of attending to the whole range of individual needs in a classroom.

Another common reaction is that the list represents a negative view of pupils with learning difficulties emphasising, as it does, what they cannot do. We accept that it is important to recognise what such pupils *can* do. For example, Professor Blackman has described such pupils as the 'vanishing handicapped' in the sense that although they have difficulties at school they often lead perfectly successful lives running jobs and personal relationships as well (or as badly) as academically far more successful pupils. His general observation is well supported by empirical data (e.g. Ashman, 1984). However, we would not accept that, even as it stands, this list of characteristics is a cause for pessimism. The key feature of many of the characteristics listed above is that there is every reason to suppose that children can be helped to change. The detailed finding from studies based on information processing models (which are merely outlined above) offer a basis for thoughtful intervention on the part of the teacher, not a rationale for despair. However, as Blackman and Lin (1984) point out, at present this is more a leap of faith than an empirically established fact.

OTHER TYPES OF DIFFERENCES

Physical differences

In this section we will discuss physical differences amongst pupils which are the consequences of temporary injury or illness, long-term physical or sensory handicaps, or chronic medical difficulties. We suggest that it is not the more dramatic aspects of some of these conditions (for example, the diabetic coma or the epileptic seizure) that present teachers with their major professional challenge. Certainly, as teachers, we should be able to carry out routine first-aid procedures. We should know when medical help should be summoned and how this can most effectively be done in our own particular school circumstances. We should be aware of straightforward ways of reducing the likelihood of these dramatic incidents (e.g. by allowing the child with diabetes to eat in class when necessary) and of ways of reducing the seriousness of any consequences of such incidents (e.g. by assigning an adult specifically to watch over a child with epilepsy during a swimming session). We should be alert to behaviour which might be of value to the child's doctors either in refining diagnosis or monitoring changed treatment regimes and should know how to report these observations.

Time needs to be taken to acquire the necessary knowledge and expertise about such issues in general terms. Liaison will be required with doctors, and other health professionals such as occupational therapists and speech therapists, both about these general aspects and about the particular needs of an individual pupil. In connection with particular pupils, advice will certainly be needed from the parents who are recognised as often having considerable knowledge and expertise in the day-to-day management of the physical and medical problems of their offspring. These are not trivial matters, however, neither are they

enormously complex. The teacher is not expected to become a medical expert, but simply to take the kind of care that a well-informed and caring parent would. What *is* complex for the teacher, is how to analyse and act upon the educational and psychological differences which might be associated with physical conditions. It is these consequent educational and psychological characteristics which affect learning which are the teacher's main professional concern.

To continue with the examples of diabetes and epilepsy, teachers need to think of how to take account of the fact that a pupil's drug regime, while largely preventing major incidents, may have side effects which hinder learning. They also need to act on knowledge of features of the handicapping condition itself. For example, the pupil with epilepsy may have quite frequent periods of altered consciousness that pass almost unnoticed in the classroom; the pupil with diabetes may become drowsy as a result of fluctuations in blood sugar level which even the best treatment may be unable to eliminate completely. These are not dramatic consequences of the conditions or their treatment, but they may well have more bearing on the pupil's learning than the occasional seizure (Postlethwaite and Hackney, 1988).

In more general terms, the educational differences which may be associated with physical conditions will cover aspects of what the pupil knows and understands, as well as what he or she can do. First we shall consider some ways in which physical conditions can affect what pupils know and understand. One obvious problem is that sensory handicaps will alter the range of pupil's experiences of the world and may reduce the opportunity for them to construct their personal understanding of phenomena in the ways that teachers are likely to expect. Even if alternative ways of exploring the environment provide rich insights for, say, a partially-sighted pupil who has a highly-developed sense of touch, teachers may not be able to understand and use these insights, and may expect other patterns of understanding which are not readily available without the use of normal sight. A somewhat different problem accompanies a condition like arthritis which may extend the time taken up by normal routines such as dressing, may reduce the range of pleasurable play activities because of limited mobility, and may tire the child. In these ways informal learning experiences are inevitably changed and opportunities for formal learning may be reduced (if, for example, essential physiotherapy also takes place during normal school time). In consequence of problems like these, children with physical difficulties may have a different knowledge base from that of their normal peers. They may know less of some things; they may know more about others (e.g. more about issues related to their condition, more about themselves, more about interpersonal relationships, and perhaps, if their condition has provided long blocks of time which the pupil has chosen to use in reading, more about some school topics). If we are to help such children to leave school without an educational handicap to add to their physical problems, it is essential that we seek to understand what they already know and that we find ways to use what they already know, recognising that their different experiences will present us both with constraints and opportunities for encouraging learning. It is also essential that we try to provide circumstances which will enable them to build aspects of understanding which might not readily be available to them without help. Medical colleagues and parents may be able to offer guidance in where to begin on these tasks, but essentially they lie within the professional domain of the teacher.

When we think about educational differences in terms of what pupils can *do*, there are again some obvious implications of physical difficulties. Partial sight, or cerebral palsy might be expected to limit pupils' abilities to manipulate apparatus in a science experiment; hearing loss may have safety implications for the science laboratory. Nevertheless, through the use of special equipment

such as that which might be used by a similarly handicapped person in their kitchen at home, through sensitive sharing of tasks amongst handicapped and non-handicapped pupils in group work, through the services of a classroom assistant, or through the advice of an occupational therapist, a teacher might help pupils with these problems to get very much involved in practical activity and to learn much of what is expected of normal peers. Certainly the fact that such a pupil may not be able to do *everything* in a practical task should not be taken as an indication that he or she is incapable of *any* involvement. Again, it is our responsibility as teachers to explore ways of reducing the limits which pupils' physical conditions set on the activities in which they can engage. It is also their responsibility to ensure that imaginative teaching is matched by imaginative assessment so that a pupil who can, say, identify relevant variables, design an experimental protocol, and analyse and interpret results is given recognition for these aspects of practical science even though lack of the fine motor control might mean that someone else had to connect up the circuit and plot the graphs.

As well as directly relevant educational differences in what a child might know, understand and can do, *psychological* differences in abilities and attitudes may accompany physical handicaps. For example, low IQ can be associated with cerebral palsy. It is, however, interesting to note that very many conditions (including the more common ones found in mainstream schools, such as asthma, diabetes and simple epilepsy) are accompanied by the normal distribution of IQ scores (Male and Thompson, 1985). It is therefore essential that teachers avoid the assumption that physical disabilities are necessarily related to low IQ.

Perhaps the more generally relevant area of psychological difference is that of pupils' attitudes. Crucial, here, are their attitudes to themselves, to their disability, to the reactions of others to their problems and, in cases such as muscular dystrophy, to such matters as their increasing dependence on others, the progressive nature of their disease and their significantly shortened life expectancy. In taking account of such factors, teachers can expect helpful advice from health professionals, parents, and perhaps especially, from educational psychologists. Nevertheless there remain significant educational problems which only the teacher can solve. Identifying and acting upon these is perhaps a good example of Warnock's comment that special needs present teachers with intellectual challenges of the highest order (DES, 1978).

We suggest, then, that by analysing physical differences in terms of their educational and psychological characteristics, we can begin to identify ways of responding to pupils that can maximise their learning. We can also be alerted to situations where physical differences really have no educational significance beyond the need for appropriate knowledge of 'first aid' of the kind we discussed earlier, to prevent or respond to occasional medical emergencies. We should be as willing to try to help physically handicapped pupils avoid the effects of any consequent educational and psychological handicaps as we are to help other pupils whose unfavourable educational and psychological attributes are not linked to a physical handicap. We should certainly be very wary of assuming that physical handicap *in itself* will set limits on what a pupil can achieve.

Social differences in the classroom

These are differences in the ways in which pupils behave in the social circumstances of the classroom. They are, for example, differences in the extent to which they are inclined to ask questions of the teacher, to answer the teacher's questions, or to express an opinion to the teacher, to individual peers or to the class. They also include differences in such things as pupils' willingness to get involved in group work, to respect the views of others, to express their own views and to take the lead where appropriate.

Such differences may relate to educational characteristics (such as what the pupil knows) and clearly relate to the psychological characteristics of motivation, personality and attitude which we have discussed above. Indeed, they might be seen as some of the more obvious expressions of these underlying characteristics. However, they do not stand in a one-to-one relationship to those characteristics in the sense that similar observed classroom behaviour may be related to very different characteristics in different pupils. For example, one pupil who chooses not to contribute to a class discussion may not understand the work which is being done, another may be introverted, another may have a low achievement motivation, and another may have a negative attitude to the subject or to school. These pupils would call for very different responses from a teacher determined to encourage their learning to as great an extent as possible.

Therefore, there will not necessarily be a direct link between observed social differences and teaching tactics. The more helpful view may be that extremes of social differences in the classroom are helpful signals to the teacher that further investigation of that particular pupil will be needed so that appropriate teaching can be devised.

Socio-economic and cultural differences

With cultural differences – and we include here differences related to factors such as race and gender, and to socio-economic background within any given race – the position is similar to that with physical handicaps, but even more complex.

Cultural differences can be expected to result in educational differences in that they will affect pupils in terms of the experiences they have and therefore the explanations of experience they construct for themselves. Cultural differences have also been shown to be related to psychological differences. For example, the link between social class and IQ has frequently been explored. From an overview of five studies conducted between 1937 and 1973 in USA, France and Scotland, Schiff and Lewontin (1986) conclude that the mean difference in IQ scores between children of high and low socio-economic status (SES) was 13 points. (In this comparison the high SES group consisted of the top 10 per cent of the SES scale; the low SES group was the bottom 50 per cent of that scale.) However they do point out that there is enormous variation in IQ scores within each social group so that social class accounts for only about 20 per cent of the variance in IQ so that simplistic arguments about IQ and class are difficult to substantiate. Furthermore, cultural differences may affect pupils in terms of their explanations for success and failure (which may, in a minority group for example, stress issues of prejudice which do not feature in the explanations of children from majority groups), they may affect pupils' attitudes to subjects (e.g. they may affect girls' views of the value of physical sciences), they may colour pupils' attitudes to teachers and to school generally. Also, they may affect pupils' problem solving abilities and their self-image as learners. For example, Feuertein et al. (1980) makes the point that cultural groups differ in the extent to which adults act as mediators for children's learning, structuring, organising and limiting their experiences so that they learn and come to recognise that they can learn.

In so far as these educational and psychological attributes matter, then cultural background matters, in terms of educational performance. Again, as in the case of physical handicap we see every reason to want to help pupils overcome any unfavourable elements in these characteristics, in much the same way that one would without the cultural link.

One might, therefore be tempted to ignore the cultural source of such educational and psychological differences and treat them just on their own merits. However, we have already discussed the point that different socio-economic and cultural groups may value education differently, and may seek different outcomes from it for their children. These differences will also matter. A controversial issue is how far we should respect these cultural differences even when they conflict with our own philosophy – e.g. how far should a teacher committed to equality of educational outcome for boys and girls in the UK education system, accept the different educational goals sought by some Asian families for their male and female offspring? In whatever way we answer that question in theory, we must recognise that our treatment of those educational and psychological differences that are rooted in cultural variety will be a practical statement of our, perhaps unconscious, solution. If our actions are to carry the

force that we intend, and if they are to avoid implications with which we would not wish to associate ourselves, then we should analyse the cultural source of some individual differences and plan our responses accordingly.

Furthermore, we should remember the possibility of bias in relation to cultural differences. The relatively weak links between IQ and class that we have already mentioned are accompanied by the fact that the prevalence of some educational outcomes is highly dependent on social class, high social class students being some 10 times more likely than low social class students to gain entry to university; low social class students being far more likely to be assigned to remedial classes (Schiff and Lewontin, 1986). The scale of these differences suggests that, even in present schools where IQ is related to outcome, IQ × Class correlations do not fully account for differential educational performance of pupils from different classes. Certainly one explanation could be that the pupils' different views of the value and purpose of education compound the effects of IQ difference. It could also be that teachers' views about, and expectations of, pupils from different cultures and classes, have an effect. There could also be cultural or class bias in the institutions and procedures of the education system. If we think only about the educational and psychological differences within pupils from different cultures we risk overlooking these other, possibly significant factors.

A further risk in omitting cultural differences from our analysis is that not all cultural influences on educational and psychological characteristics should be assumed to be unhelpful. We should be quick to capitalise on opportunities for successful learning which are generated by cultural attributes. Of course, this may not be easy to do for we run the risk of being trapped by our own culture and expectations, but it is important to be alert to the possibility.

Other relevant considerations

The analysis presented above of various *kinds* of pupil characteristics is important for, as we have seen, there are differences in the relationship between these characteristics and educational achievement and these need to be taken into account in planning teaching. However, there are other ways of analysing the differences amongst pupils, which tend to cut across the types of variation which we have so far discussed. These are considerations of stability, locus of control, pervasiveness and value.

Stability

Individual differences can vary in their stability. Some persist, relatively unchanged for many years and can affect pupils' lives throughout their time in school, and beyond; some characteristics, at the other extreme, vary from day to day. It is important to note that the severity of the problem faced by a pupil does not necessarily depend on its stability. Some short-term problems such as those associated with a traumatic event at home can be very severe. However, the treatment of a problem must take account of its stability. For example, very temporary characteristics may require no intervention on the part of the teacher as a change to a more desirable state can be expected to come about of its own accord; some potentially short-term problems may call for swift action to bring about the desired change in order to avoid the development of more persistent consequences; entirely stable characteristics call for attempts to circumvent their effects rather than attempts to change the characteristics themselves.

Generally, educational differences tend to be relatively unstable in that what people know, understand and can do change constantly as they learn new things. Psychological characteristics tend to be more stable – indeed to some extent they depend on their stability for their power to explain behaviour – but some such as IQ are more open to change than is often imagined and those which are closest to educational differences (such as academic self image) tend to share their potentially temporary nature.

Locus of control

Closely linked to the concept of stability is that of the extent to which teachers and pupils are able

to control whether or not a characteristic changes: the extent to which the characteristic is alterable. Some characteristics, like cerebral palsy may be long-term and outside anyone's control given the present state of medical science; some, like a broken bone, may be temporary, but essentially outside the control of the teacher; some, like IQ, may be fairly stable but open to some change if the teacher employs appropriate strategies of kinds which we shall discuss later; some, like the lack of a piece of learning which is a prerequisite for some new learning task, lie very much within the teacher's expected and normal sphere of influence.

The stability and alterability of characteristics will affect whether it is wise to tackle them within a remedial model where change of the characteristic is the aim, or whether one should seek instead ways to enable learning to continue despite the characteristic which is itself unchanged.

Pervasiveness

Some characteristics of pupils are quite pervasive in that they affect all aspects of the pupils' work in school. Others appear only in a very restricted range of contexts. Differences of this second kind may, perhaps, be more usefully seen as problems of the context than as problems of the children themselves. One consequence of this is that their educational impact may be open to change by change in the context alone. Another implication is that context-specific characteristics should never be allowed to limit the pupil's access to parts of the curriculum for which they are not relevant. Something of this thinking lies behind pressure to integrate physically handicapped pupils into mainstream schools so that they can study the full range of subjects for which their physical problems are not a bar – opportunities which might not exist in a small special school for physically handicapped pupils without, say, science facilities. A final point is that remedies for more pervasive characteristics may sometimes be applied in a very context-specific way, and may in consequence be of severely limited benefit to the child. Some of the ineffectiveness of remedial provision for poor readers may fall into this trap by failing to address the differences between reading in, say, science and the reading of novels. If the reading problem is pervasive, the treatment may be too specific to help across the whole scope of the problem.

Implicit value judgements

The very concept of altering a pupil implies that the characteristics under consideration are not only alterable but also undesirable. In contrast, the concept of finding ways round a pupil's problem so that it no longer limits their learning does not necessarily carry such implication. Often, though not always, there would be widespread consensus about any such value judgements; but clarity of thinking about individual differences does require a disentangling of people's described characteristics from judgements about their desirability or about what the people need.

SUMMARY

To summarise the argument so far: there are educational, psychological, physical, social and cultural differences amongst pupils. For each of these we should be concerned to establish the stability and pervasiveness of the characteristic, to consider the extent to which change in this characteristic can be controlled by the teacher, and to analyse any implicit value judgements that may accompany our thinking about the characteristics. We should remember that educational differences are the only ones which inevitably have effects on educational outcome. Other differences can sometimes be shown empirically to have such effects in the particular circumstances in which the empirical work was done.

This framework for thinking about pupils generates a very significant challenge: namely that of planning a response to all the different characteristics which we have discussed. It is this challenge that we will attempt to meet in subsequent chapters.

CHAPTER 3

Responding to pupil differences: some possible teaching tactics

In this chapter, we are concerned with the teaching tactics which can be used to respond to the individual characteristics of our pupils so that each can be helped to learn science effectively. The account of pupil characteristics from Chapter 2 can be helpful here as it reminds us of the range of possible factors which might be influencing a pupil's learning and therefore of the range of approaches to teaching that we might need to devise. Because of the wide range of differences identified in Chapter 2, this is a long chapter. It has two main sections: one is concerned with tactics related to educational differences; the other is relevant to psychological differences. The chapter begins with a brief discussion of some broader issues and ends with some specific comments about tactics which are relevant to able pupils.

REMEDIATION AND CIRCUMVENTION

Chapter 2 can be used to justify – and indeed can be said to require – two broad approaches to pupils' difficulties: the remedial approach and the circumvention approach. The argument that was developed there suggests that, in analysing a pupil's problem, we must decide if it is a persistent or potentially short-term problem, and if it is the latter we must decide if it is within our control to bring about change. If it is, we must make a value judgement about whether the characteristic which generates the problem is undesirable. Though this may rarely be problematic, it may require some very hard thinking where, for example, cultural differences are involved. Where potentially short-term, undesirable characteristics lying within our sphere of influence are identified, we can think in terms of trying a remedial approach designed to correct the difficulty which the pupil has. Where the problem relates to characteristics which are permanent, or to temporary characteristics which nevertheless lie outside our sphere of influence, or where the characteristics cannot properly be seen as undesirable, we must think of ways of circumventing the problem so that the pupil can be helped to learn despite the continued presence of the characteristic. There is, of course, nothing here to suggest a return to crude labelling of *pupils* as 'remedial pupils'. 'Remedial' is a type of teaching tactic, not a type of pupil. This explicit distinction between remedial tactics and tactics of circumvention is essential if we are to proceed on a firm footing. Within each of these broad approaches we have then to be able to identify or devise tactics which are relevant to the very different educational, psychological, physical, social and cultural categories of pupil difference.

Some points of simplification

The requirements outlined above might, with justification, be regarded as a significant challenge. However there are some opportunities for simplification. First, some of the points which were raised in Chapter 2 have greater relevance to our attitudes to pupils than to the tactics which we should use to teach them effectively. This reduces the range of specific tactics with which we need to be concerned. Secondly, we rarely have to devise tactics from scratch. Many appropriate tactics already exist and are well documented in the literature (e.g. Harvey et al., 1982; Bulman, 1985; Raban and Postlethwaite, 1988; Montgomery, 1990). What is necessary is that such tactics are readily available to teachers and, especially, that they are analysed to ensure that we know what kinds of tactics they are, and what kinds of problems they might address. Finally, a commitment to teach with regard to individual differences does not mean that we have to resource all lessons at the same time. The work which we do will be of long-standing value in the sense that the procedures which we devise will be reusable with other classes and in later years. It follows that an individual science teacher or a school science department could work towards greater sensitivity to individual needs over a period of years concentrating development on, for example, different year groups or different aspects of the 11–16 science curriculum at different times.

It is largely this set of simplifying ideas which will provide a structure for this chapter. Though, the discussion above has stressed the issue of learning *difficulties*, I will keep the needs of more able pupils in mind as I try to address the various points. In addition, I shall end the chapter with some specific comments about able pupils.

Teacher attitudes to pupil differences

Some of the points raised in Chapter 2 offer little in the way of direct guidance on how we should teach a pupil but are nevertheless of great value to teachers as they can help to shape our attitudes to pupils. One point of this kind is the argument that a single-factor model of intelligence based on IQ should be replaced by a multifactorial model in which intelligence is represented by several different aptitudes which are only slightly correlated. In such a model a pupil might have quite high scores on some aptitude, but lower scores on others. This pattern of scores might well produce a low general ability score, and yet the pupil's areas of strength may be quite specifically linked to our subject and could be expected to lead to sound performance in that subject. It is therefore important that we keep an open mind about performance in our subject, when we hear some general information about a pupil's characteristics. (This can have a significant impact, for it might well make us very suspicious of calls to base the academic organisation of our school on streaming which places pupils in the same teaching groups for all subjects on the basis of some general measure of ability or achievement.) Of course, keeping an open mind and waiting to be surprised by a pupil's success will not be enough: we will need to think carefully about our teaching methods in order to encourage the pupil to make use of his or her strengths. It may not be easy to see how the multi-dimensional model of intelligence can help us to design such teaching, but that does not weaken its value in influencing our attitudes.

A similar point – indeed, perhaps the key point – is that the educational significance of most pupil characteristics has to be demonstrated empirically. It is not a logical necessity. As we pointed out in Chapter 2, this means that links between a pupil characteristic and educational performance which *have* been established, can only be assumed to hold in the circumstances in which they were determined: there is no reason to assume that they must necessarily hold in all other circumstances. This, in turn, implies that when a pupil with some particular characteristic experiences difficulties in our lessons we should be spurred to consider and modify our teaching so as to break the link between the characteristic and achievement. We should not too readily accept the alternative view that the link is such as to make the pupil's difficulties inevitable.

This has far-reaching consequences for it also implies that we should be suspicious of teaching which too readily sets lower expectations for some pupils on the grounds that they have some particular characteristic. Even if there is evidence that such pupils often perform badly in relation to the normal aims we have for education, this cannot be interpreted as showing that they will *necessarily* perform badly in relation to those aims by whatever methods they are taught. This, in turn suggests that we should be slow to alter the aims and objectives of education for pupils with particular characteristics, especially as alternative aims often carry less weight outside school, for example in areas such as the employment market. There is surely no justification for denying pupils access to the normal, more influential educational goals just because in some circumstances they do not achieve these as easily as some of their peers. Indeed, to do so would seem to offend against natural justice. This position is nicely summarised by Cronbach and Snow (1977, p. 522):

> ... shunting some students into a 'non-academic' curriculum cannot be tolerated, so long as proficiencies formerly considered 'academic' are necessary for most kinds of success and participation in society. Educators have to invent methods to open opportunity to persons who would not attain traditional goals in traditional ways.

Of course, the argument that a different teaching tactic *could* help pupils with low IQ to achieve more than we might be tempted to expect, leads one immediately to ask whether there is evidence that this has actually been achieved. Several of the tactics that can be used with pupils who have learning difficulties have been carefully researched and can provide affirmative answers to this question. Some of these are discussed later in this chapter. However, at this stage, I would like to refer to direct and believable evidence which can be found in a splendidly titled book *Yes, they can!* (Weber, 1974). In a chapter entitled 'For those who believe that adolescent slow learners cannot think', Weber describes his work with a group of nine pupils whose average WISC score (across the verbal and performance components) ranged from 68 to 88. He also describes a set of five problems which he set them. (An example of a problem is: 'A farmer has three pigs which he keeps in triangular pens. The pens are made of gates (one for each side) and the gates are all the same length. He can afford to buy one more pig, but he cannot afford any more gates. Move the gates around until you make four pens that are all the same size.') To help the pupils, the problems were first presented orally, pupils were given small sticks to manipulate to help them work out a solution, and pupils were given the opportunity, as a group, to explore the general features of the situation (e.g. how the original pig pens were made) before the actual problem (penning one extra pig) was posed for them to work on individually.

This description of Weber's approach offers us clues to a possible teaching approach to help pupils with low IQ to solve problems. However, more significant at this stage of the argument is his evaluation of the effects produced. Since nine pupils each did five such problems, 45 answers were possible: only one was recorded as 'no solution offered' and only four were inaccurate. The time taken to solve the problems ranged from 13 seconds to 10 minutes 6 seconds, indicating both considerable speed on the part of some pupils in their problem solving and considerable tenacity on the part of others.

Weber goes on to say that he tried similar problems in a small-scale comparison between university students and his 'slow learning' pupils. The pupils solved the problems more quickly than the university students. He accepts that this may reflect the amount of practice that the pupils had in this kind of problem solving, but it certainly indicates that pupils with low IQs can solve problems that are non-trivial to people who are traditionally reckoned to be very much brighter. In discussing Weber's work with my own university students I have sometimes also set them Weber's problems to do and I have also found that university graduates were often slower than Weber's group of pupils in coming up with solutions. The extent to which the students expressed surprise, even disbelief, at the comparison of their efforts with those of the pupils may indicate just how strongly we tend to believe that low IQ pupils simply *cannot* do things.

The evidence from Weber's work, coupled with the theoretical justification (presented in Chapter 2) for the view that correlations between IQ and achievement are not inevitable, can perhaps lead to the weakening of this attitude. This can, in turn, encourage us to search for teaching tactics which match the characteristics of our pupils in ways

that help them all (those with low IQ and those with other characteristics which are generally seen as unfavourable) to achieve significant goals. The results of more formal studies of the effects of the specific teaching tactics which I will report later, will, I hope, continue the process of attitude change.

In the next two major sections of this chapter, I will suggest some tactics for responding to many of the pupil characteristics discussed in Chapter 2, and will try to distinguish between 'remedial' and 'circumvention' approaches so that appropriate tools can be used in any given situation. The next section will concentrate on tactics relevant to educational differences. The following section will cover tactics relevant to psychological differences. In both sections I shall draw heavily on existing ideas in the literature. So much can be found there that I shall not even attempt a comprehensive catalogue of tactics. I shall, however, try to give a broad perspective, quoting examples in each area, together with references to sources where much more detail can be found.

TACTICS RELATED TO EDUCATIONAL DIFFERENCES

I pointed out, in Chapter 2, that there were two major sources of general insight into what pupils know, understand and can do: the Assessment of Performance Unit (APU) reports can indicate areas of the science curriculum in which pupils might be expected to have difficulty, and the research on pupils' alternative frameworks (notably that of the Children's Learning in Science Project) can indicate the ways in which pupils might be expected to think about some science concepts. These two sources do not replace the need for us to enquire in detail into the understanding and

alternative frameworks of our specific pupils, but as we plan lessons to take account of our pupils' educational differences we can use these general sources in different ways.

Tactics related to differences in pupils' understanding of accepted scientific ideas

The APU reports give us clear indications of some areas in which pupils can be expected to have difficulty in our lessons. As an example of the way in which such information might be used, the APU survey of 13-year olds (APU, 1982) reveals that about 70 per cent of these pupils gained no marks on a question which asked them to explain, in terms of particle theory, the fact that the pressure in a car tyre increases during a journey. At the same time, some 4 per cent gave a full qualitative explanation of this effect. With this information in mind, we can appreciate the need to return to the basics of the particle model of matter with older pupils in order to clarify its main points before building on them in some new teaching. We can also see the importance of planning some extension work for the 4 per cent to do so that the lessons spent on this are not wasted time for them.

Furthermore, the details of the answers which pupils gave in the APU survey can suggest the kinds of points which our new treatment of the model might emphasise, and can give pointers to how we might change our earlier treatment of the topic so that the 70 per cent are better able to grasp the topic in the first place. For example, 8 per cent of 13-year olds said that the particles expand or increase as the tyre gets warm. These errors might encourage us to draw explicit attention to the distinction between what is happening at the macroscopic level and what we believe to be happening at the microscopic level. It might encourage us to say: 'The particles themselves don't get bigger. It's just that they move about faster and bang into the tyre at higher speed creating a bigger force – just like a faster moving ball creates a bigger force on you if it hits you.' We might also look for concrete experiences for pupils which will reinforce this message. In addition, we might draw from the APU findings the conclusion that pupils tend not to string their ideas together into a logically developed explanation and might therefore decide to spend time pointing out the characteristics of such an explanation. The APU findings can then directly inform the way we teach.

This example, based directly on the APU reports is very neat, but risks stating the obvious. Lessons which we will need to teach will rarely be as closely linked to APU results as was the case here. Nevertheless, APU findings can still

be useful in helping us to address educational differences. This is because the APU results can give us insights into pupils' understanding of background concepts which are relevant as necessary precursors to a wide range of lessons that may not be focused directly on those concepts. For example, many practical lessons will involve the use of graphs. Thus, if we are about to teach the concept of half-life to GCSE pupils by plotting activity against time and then inspecting the properties of the graph, it is helpful to know from APU that scale interpolation gave rise to problems for the average and below average performance groups in their survey of 15-year olds. Alerted by this specific finding, we might, in advance of our lesson on half-life, design a homework task or classroom activity which will give us insights into our own pupils' abilities to interpolate graph scales. With information from this enquiry in mind, we can plan how to give attention to this issue with the class as a whole before expecting pupils to use the graphs effectively, or how to take up the issue with individuals as we work with them during the lesson. Thus the APU results can help us to focus our attention, during a 'diagnosis' as well as a teaching phase, on aspects of the interpretation of graphs that might hinder our pupils in their learning of a new concept.

To summarise, since differences in prior understanding necessarily affect new learning, we must clearly plan our lessons in ways that take account of what pupils must already know. A first step is to decide what the necessary prerequisites are for the new teaching we are planning. Once this is done, APU surveys can often provide at least partial information on how much of this necessary prior knowledge pupils in general can reasonably be expected to have, and on the kinds of difficulties that might be expected. This can help us to target our diagnostic enquiry into our *own* pupils' current understanding, and increase the probability that it will provide us with useful information. Such diagnostic enquiries might then be made through homework activities, or through a review of pupils' written work, or through a structured class discussion in which pupils can be encouraged to talk about the topic in ways that reveal something of their thinking. The results of such enquiry can affect our lesson planning for the group, and the ways in which we work with individuals within that group. It is worth noting a helpful simplifying point: planning of this kind will usually cover a *series* of lessons rather than just an individual lesson. This greatly reduces the planning workload and makes the whole enterprise much more realistic.

This sequence presupposes, of course, that we can determine what is needed as prior understanding. Very often our subject expertise and experience of teaching pupils will be entirely adequate to enable us to do this. However, we will find that pupils sometimes have difficulties in learning even after we have planned our lessons to take account of the variations in what they already know about the expected precursors for the new learning. In such circumstances it is possible that we have overlooked some necessary precursor and that pupils who have difficulty with this are therefore unable to benefit from our teaching. It is then helpful to have some basis for a closer analysis of what the necessary precursors are. One set of ideas which can help in carrying out such an analysis is Gagné's work on hierarchies (of which a useful summary can be found in Gagné and Briggs, 1974). By drawing our attention to different kinds of precursors for learning, Gagné widens our view in ways that might be helpful in planning work for a whole class; by indicating that some precursors are very basic, he can alert us to things which we might otherwise continue to overlook even when thinking hard about a particular pupil's difficulties. These points will, I hope, be clarified in the discussion which follows.

Gagné proposes that problem solving in the intellectual domain requires the use of rules which themselves require an understanding of concepts, which in turn require the pupil to make discriminations between things they see or hear. These discriminations require the pupil to use more basic intellectual skills, but these will rarely be the concern of secondary school staff – even those in special needs departments. Gagné argues that this hierarchy can be applied to any subject matter.

The meaning of the terms can be illustrated by a simple example. Suppose a pupil is to interpret the results of a chemical test using litmus paper. To do this successfully, the pupil must be able to: *discriminate* between blue and red; have the *concept* of acid and alkali; know and be able to apply the *rule* that acid turns blue litmus red and that an alkali turns red litmus blue. Faced with a pupil who has difficulty with this task, a thoughtful chemistry teacher is likely to check up on the pupil's understanding of the rule and may explore their grasp of the concepts but may well overlook the need to establish whether the pupil can make the necessary discrimination. Gagné's model helps to alert us to the need to explore the whole range of necessary precursors for the task we have set. We will now explore these elements in more detail.

Gagné describes *discriminations* as the 'capability of making different responses to stimuli that differ from each other along one or more physical dimensions'. We have already considered the relevance of visual discrimination of colours. Another example involves auditory discrimination: a necessary precursor to the ability to test the hypothesis that short objects produce higher notes than long objects is the ability to discriminate pitch. This again indicates the kind of very basic thing it would be easy for a science teacher to overlook if a pupil was having difficulty with the scientific hypothesis. If Gagné's work was limited to the role of helping us to consider the importance of such discriminations it would be of value. However, it goes further: it indicates ways in which pupils can be helped to learn to discriminate. At this very basic level, his advice relates closely to classical stimulus–response learning theory:

- he suggests that work on discriminations might begin by asking the pupil to consider stimuli which are very different and easy to discriminate (e.g. notes more than an octave apart) and move on to those where the differences are more subtle
- he draws attention to the need to reinforce pupils' responses, distinguishing clearly between correct and incorrect discriminations, by giving pupils simple, familiar, pleasurable activities to

follow correct discriminations – activities which are not given following wrong discriminations

- he points out the importance of giving this reinforcement within a short time span of the discrimination being made, and the importance of repeating the exercise several times

This kind of work might well take place in a one-to-one setting such as a withdrawal session in the special needs department, or as an individualised activity in the science laboratory with a classroom assistant. In these contexts, reinforcement activities can perhaps be built in to a game where correct discriminations allow the pupil to move a further step round the board, or to have the next part of a picture revealed, or whatever. It would not be difficult to enlist the help of the computer in providing the pupil both with discrimination tasks and with rewards.

Concepts enable us to group a number of things together into a class on the basis of some key characteristic(s), even though they may differ considerably in other ways. The concept of 'current' enables us to group together the superficially very different phenomena of a $1\,\mu A$ current in a semiconductor, a $300\,A$ current in a car starter motor, an alternating current, a direct current, a nerve impulse, a movement of electrons in a wire and of ions in a liquid on the basis that they all involve moving charge. This is useful as we can predict the properties of all these different currents on the basis of experiments done on some examples of the class. Gagné sub-divides concepts into concrete concepts and defined concepts. Concrete concepts are concepts of which examples can be identified directly by observation: 'girl' is a concrete concept; so are notions of object position such as 'above' or 'between'. Defined concepts are more abstract in that they involve relationships: 'sister' is a defined concept in the sense that one has to understand the family links between people to identify whether someone is an example of the concept or not. The decision cannot be based solely on observation. The distinction between concrete and defined concepts sometimes seems rather slippery and Gagné makes the helpful point that one can appreciate some

concepts at both levels. 'Circle' can be a concrete concept if a pupil judges a given figure on its general appearance in order to decide if it is an example of the class 'circle' or not. However, it can also be a defined concept where the pupil understands that a circle is the set of points which are all a fixed distance from a given point. The concrete version of 'circle' might serve pupils well in many school situations, but it might leave them unable to cope with work in maths or science which relied on the formal properties of a circle. There are many opportunities for confusion if the pupil is coping with work on the basis of a concrete concept whereas the teacher imagines that he or she is using the defined concept. There are also clearly links between these views and Piaget's notions of concrete and formal operational thought.

Gagné argues that pupils learn concrete concepts if they can already make the necessary discriminations and if they are given lots of examples of the concept and lots of non-examples. If too few examples are presented, the pupil's view of the concept may be too narrow (e.g. if all examples of 'square' are open line drawings the pupil might fail to recognise a square filled with a pattern as an example of that concept; if convection is always shown in liquids, pupils may not see that it also applies to gases). Similarly, if too few non-examples are presented the pupil's view of the concept may be too wide (e.g. she or he may include a rectangle in the class of 'squares', or may consider stirring to be an example of convection).

Defined concepts make greater demands on pupils and give scope for different kinds of confusion between the teacher and learner. If we teach that 'current is the flow of electric charge', the pupil, in order to learn that defined concept has to be able to recall the concept of charge and the concept of flow. If the pupil's notion of charge does not include the idea of positive and negative, ideas about current in liquids are likely to be puzzling; if the pupil's idea of flow does not include the idea of backwards and forwards motion then alternating current is going to present problems. We may not wish to address all of these issues when we first define current, but we will need to remember that later difficulties with, say, alternating current, may relate back to some partial understanding of one of the component concepts. There is another, and perhaps more interesting problem: namely that a pupil can repeat the verbal string 'current is a flow of charge' without knowing the meaning of the concept of 'current' at all. Rather than asking for definitions to test pupils' understanding, we need to get the pupil to use the concept, e.g. by suggesting a model for current.

Other insights into the learning of concepts are summarised by Howard (1987). He discusses the value of:

- explicitly teaching the defining features of a concept as well as presenting examples and non-examples
- discussing the irrelevant features (e.g. with squares, whether they contain a pattern or not)
- drawing attention to superordinate concepts (e.g. 'mechanisms of heat transfer' is a concept which is superordinate to 'convection' in the sense that it is the more general concept into which 'convection' fits as one of several examples)
- listing subordinate concepts (e.g. listing mammals, fish, reptiles, amphibians, insects, birds as subordinate to the concept 'animal')

He also discusses the interesting idea that potentially confusing concepts (especially concepts at the same level of generality) should be taught at the same time and that the elements of concept teaching outlined above should be used to draw explicit attention to the similarities and differences between these concepts and their range of application. This idea would, for example, encourage us to teach the concepts of momentum and energy at the same time during a more formal treatment of motion, say for 15- or 16-year old pupils, rather than separating their treatment by a term or more 'in order to reduce confusion'. Another, closely associated idea is that of the concept map which is a diagrammatic representation of the kinds of relationships amongst concepts which are described above. A brief, and helpful discussion of the use of concept maps in science is provided by Brodie (1991).

To return to Gagné's hierarchy: at the top, Gagné places 'rules'. These cover a wide range of human behaviour. Pupils use rules (though they may not be able to state them explicitly) when they construct sentences; they use rules when they classify a cell seen under a microscope as either an animal or plant cell, or calculate the unbalanced force acting on an object using $F = ma$. As is clear from the example of animal and plant cells, the definitions of defined concepts are themselves one kind of rule.

Once they are learnt, simple rules can be sequenced by the pupil (with or without help from the teacher) so as to offer a solution to a novel problem. The sequence is then remembered and used to solve similar problems in the future. Some rules that pupils construct govern their own thinking (e.g. to remember a French word, try to find a similar English word that has a related meaning and remember the trio of words together as in *roi-royal-king*). Gagné described these as cognitive strategies.

Gagné argues that basic rule learning requires that:

- the pupils are told what they will be able to do when they have learnt the rule
- they are given help to review the concepts which are involved in the rule
- they are helped to learn the rule (either by discussion which gradually pieces the rule together or by less closely guided 'discovery learning')
- they are asked to demonstrate that they can use the rule (not merely state it) and are provided with clear feedback on their performance
- they are helped to make a verbal statement of what the rule is
- there is review of the rule a day or more after the original learning

To encourage the sequencing of rules into problem-solving strategies, Gagné suggests that the teacher should ask questions that encourage recall of the component rules and should, to a greater or lesser extent channel the pupil's thinking. At a minimum this consists in defining 'the goal of the activity (and) the general form of the solution'; it may also include providing input designed to focus the learner on particularly helpful elements of the situation.

Gagné therefore provides a system for analysing precursors to new learning, and describes specific teaching tactics designed to help pupils to acquire basic skills and understanding. However, both Gagné and APU stress the extent to which pupils know and understand the *usual* scientific explanations of phenomena. They map educational differences by showing how far pupils have come down the path of an already-defined science curriculum. The next section takes a different viewpoint.

Tactics related to differences in pupils' alternative explanations for phenomena

Research on pupils' alternative frameworks takes a different view of educational differences from that attributed to Gagné and APU above. It stresses that pupils will have their own explanations for phenomena that will work, at least to some extent, for them. It stresses that these explanations will affect the ways in which pupils react to our teaching. In this model, if we are to teach individuals effectively, we need to understand individual differences in prior understanding not so that we can go back far enough to build upon a firm base that the pupil may have, but so that we can try to change the limited, less powerful explanations that they have constructed, into the more generalisable, more powerful explanations that lie within the scope of formal science.

The research on alternative frameworks that we discussed in Chapter 2, gives insights into what pupils often think about some common scientific phenomena. If we are about to teach lessons concerned with these phenomena we may well be able to make direct use of this research, in ways that we will shortly consider, in order to make our teaching more effective for all our pupils. However, as in the case of the APU work, it is perhaps helpful to ask the more general question of how knowledge about alternative frameworks can inform a wider range of teaching.

First, it is helpful to note that research on pupils'

frameworks has identified some general characteristics which we might be able to take account of in our teaching. Osborne et al. (1983) have summarised some of these. For example, children tend to focus on direct aspects of experience rather than abstract ideas, often taking a self-centred, or at least human-centred point of view. Thus, children may find it easy to think in terms of energy when the context is personal or human activity (e.g. food is a source of energy), but may find the notion that a spring can store energy quite meaningless. The person-centred notion of energy is not generalised to provide understanding of the abstract term. In such circumstances it is little wonder that schemes of work on energy which stress the transformation of energy from one abstract form to another (e.g. chemical energy is transformed into electrical energy in a battery and then into heat and light in a bulb) have been ineffective for so many children. Such schemes sub-divide an already abstract and inaccessible idea into still more abstract sub-categories. More recent schemes of work, such as Nuffield Co-ordinated Science, which stress the transfer of energy (e.g. energy is transferred from the battery to the bulb and then into the environment) are more likely to be accessible, in part because they take account of this characteristic of pupils' own ways of thinking about energy without compromising the validity of the science which they present.

Another general finding is that pupils tend to look for specific explanations of specific events. They seem not to be worried if their explanation of one phenomenon is contradicted by their explanation of another. They tend not to seek broad generalising concepts. For example, pupils may argue that they suck liquid up a straw, that gravity causes an evacuated can to collapse and that the engines hold a plane in the air. They will not look for, nor be particularly impressed by, the notion that air pressure can explain all of these effects. They may well find the explanation of flight based on Bernoulli's principle implausible and complex compared with their simpler idea. Similarly, pupils holding the common view that objects need a force to keep them moving, may not be at all bothered by the contradiction between this and the fact (that they may also know) that there is no force in the direction of motion of the earth that keeps it moving round the sun.

Finally, Osborne et al. report that children tend to bring their increasing knowledge of the common use of words to bear on their scientific thinking. This can lead pupils to change their personal explanations, moving away from earlier correct notions to less acceptable ones. A good example is that young children will often describe a spider as an animal, whereas older children, influenced by the common link between this word and images of four-legged furry or hairy things like dogs, cats, horses and cows, may not.

Another useful general notion about children's alternative frameworks is that they tend to have three elements. Children think about an agent (some basic cause of the effect); they think about an object (something which is being acted upon); they think about an instrument (some means by which the agent acts on the object). This has two implications for a teacher wishing to explore children's thinking. First, it suggests that we need to know all three aspects of their model in order to have a full picture of it, and that if we do not know what the child is regarding as agent, instrument and object we probably have only a partial picture of their framework. Secondly it suggests that once children have identified all three aspects, they may look no further. For example, in the situation of a battery lighting a bulb, a pupil may regard the battery as agent, the bulb as object and a wire from battery to bulb as instrument. The child may then feel that all aspects of an explanation are in place and fail to notice, or to be convinced by the teacher's emphasis on, the need for a return wire from bulb to battery.

All these general insights can be useful to the teacher in the kind of way that I have illustrated in the case of APU's findings. They can help us to be alert to children generally might be thinking and therefore, when we try to discover the particular alternative frameworks of the actual pupils in our classes, they may guide our enquiries and urge us to continue until a full picture is obtained. But how might such enquiries be conducted?

Discovering pupils' alternative frameworks

If we are interested in our pupils' thinking in areas where research has already established what the common alternative frameworks are, we can make good use of written tests. Multiple-choice questions can be used, where the distractors are based on common alternative frameworks or their implications. Short-answer questions can be used, and pupils' answers analysed to reveal the nature of their thinking, rather than simply to establish the degree of match with some predetermined mark scheme. Questions that discuss a novel context may be particularly revealing (e.g. 'Describe Brownian Motion from the point of view of the smoke particle' or 'You are an electron going around a circuit in which a single battery lights two bulbs in series. Describe what happens to you in the battery, the wire, the first bulb and the second bulb. What happens after you have been through the second bulb?'). These approaches can be used with whole classes in order to guide our general approach to a topic, or on a one-to-one basis in order to help us decide how to remedy a pupil's problems with a given topic.

Another approach which can be useful with whole classes is the brainstorming technique in which pupils are encouraged to contribute as many ideas as possible about some issue such as why things float. While ideas are being collected from the class no judgements are made about their validity. If a large number of ideas are collected, it may be necessary to prioritise some for further investigation in the lesson, but this should be done as a separate stage and ideally, we should try to find opportunities to discuss the other ideas with the pupils who generated them.

Where we suspect that some idiosyncratic alternative framework is giving rise to particular difficulties for a pupil (a possibility that may be well worth considering when teaching a pupil with special educational needs who has significant learning difficulties in our subject) we may wish to explore their thinking at greater depth than can be achieved through written work or class-based brainstorming. The technique of 'interviews about instances' (Gilbert and Osborne, 1982) can be helpful for this purpose. These interviews are conducted on a one-to-one basis, and are best tape recorded so that pupils' responses can be considered at length after the event. For this reason they are better suited to the withdrawal situation and might ideally be conducted, on behalf of the science department, by scientifically qualified special needs staff should such staff exist.

Interviews about instances are concerned with a pupil's understanding of a particular concept such as 'reaction' in chemistry. The pupil is shown up to 20 cards each with a picture which either does or does not represent an example of this concept. The pictures (ideally, perhaps, colour photographs) relate largely to everyday contexts. There might, for example, be pictures of a saucepan boiling on a cooker, of a firework going off, of a car going rusty, etc. The pupil is asked whether, in their meaning of the word 'reaction', each card is or is not an instance of that concept. They are then asked to explain their reasoning. Because of the interview situation, the pupil can discuss the card, ask for clarification, and so forth, all of which can be revealing about his or her thinking. After sufficient cards have been presented, the pupil is asked to define the concept. (If they cannot, they are provided with the usual definition.) The process then continues with more cards depicting examples and non-examples of the concept in traditional science contexts (e.g. magnesium burning in oxygen in a gas jar).

The choice and order of presentation of the cards is important. The interview should start with familiar and accessible situations so as not to unsettle the pupil at first. In a research setting, the card orders used would be subjected to formal pre-test, but when interviews-about-instances are used as a diagnostic tool for the teacher, repeated use of the method should enable them, over time, to choose the most effective cards and card orders. In interviews about instances the teacher must take care to put the pupil at ease. The pupil must be assured that there is no 'right answer': that it is the pupils' own ideas that are the point of interest. The teacher must also take care to ensure that pupils are not prompted along a given line by verbal or non-verbal cues, and that negative

feedback is avoided when pupils are saying something which does match the formal scientific definition.

Of course, all such approaches have limitations. Multiple-choice questions can only reveal the extent of use of the frameworks which are embedded in the distractors. They cannot reveal that some other framework is being used by a particular pupil. Also pupils may have learnt the trick of providing the scientifically acceptable answer to the teacher in a formal test setting, while still actually believing an alternative explanation which they continue to use in less formal situations, even in science lessons. Unmotivated children may choose not to contribute to discussion-based explorations, shy pupils may not respond well to one-to-one interview situations, pupils with poor academic self-image may not feel that their ideas are worth expressing and, in most approaches, pupils' incomplete mastery of language may mask their actual thinking. Factors of this kind may be especially significant when we are exploring the alternative frameworks of pupils with special educational needs. Nevertheless, investigations of pupils' thinking can be valuable, especially if we have some clear ideas on how we might bring about change once their thinking has been made explicit. It is to this issue that we now turn.

Changing pupils' alternative frameworks (constructivist learning)

The constructivist model of learning to which concerns about alternative frameworks belong has, at its heart, the notion that pupils are active agents in their own learning, observing phenomena and constructing models to explain them. These models are remembered and used if they enable the pupil to make accurate predictions of what will happen in later circumstances in which the phenomenon may occur. As Driver (1983) points out, this active view of the learner is consistent with Piaget's theories of cognitive development, though Piaget is concerned with changes in pupils' general style of thinking (e.g. from concrete operations to formal operations) whereas constructivist views of learning in science are concerned with changes in some specific aspect of thinking about a scientific effect (e.g. a changed view on the explanation of floating). Piaget's theory rests on the notion of the pupil assimilating information (or any form of input from the environment) into an existing cognitive structure. If the new information fits the existing structure, assimilation is the end of the matter. However, from time to time information is assimilated which does not quite fit – in the sense that predictions based on the existing structure do not match the new observations or information. A period of disequilibrium then exists and it is the need to resolve this which provides the intrinsic motivation for learning. The process by which resolution is achieved is known as 'accommodation': the pupil's cognitive structure is changed in order to accommodate the new information. This change enlarges the scope and the predictive power of the pupil's thinking and is therefore a genuine advance in their learning. It is interesting to note that information which cannot be made to relate at all to a pupil's existing structure will not be assimilated, but will simply be ignored or rejected. As Driver points out, this suggests that what is needed to bring about accommodation, is new information or observation which embodies 'moderate novelty'.

The idea about changing pupils' alternative frameworks by presenting them with input which contains a moderate amount of novelty has been investigated by Nussbaum and Novick (1981) who suggested the following sequence for teaching:

- make children's alternative frameworks explicit to them (e.g. in one or more of the ways discussed above)
- present evidence that does not fit (this is the element of moderate novelty – Nussbaum and Novick call this a 'cognitive conflict')
- present the new framework based on formal science, and explain how it can account for the previous anomaly

In the science teaching context, probably the most powerful way of introducing a cognitive conflict is by presenting experimental evidence which does not fit with pupils' predictions based on their alternative frameworks. Thus, if a pupil's view is that wood floats because it is wood, presenting an experiment in which a dense hardwood sinks in alcohol will establish a cognitive conflict. To make the teaching sequence effective the anomaly has to be sufficiently powerful to engage pupils' interest. The teacher has a part here, in drawing attention to the conflict in a stimulating way ('Just a minute. Look at this. This isn't what we expected is it? Look the wood has sunk . . .'). Also, the teacher has to prevent pupils from dismissing it as 'just an oddity' (e.g. by regarding wood provided by the teacher as special and not subject to the rules of ordinary wood), and from accepting it as 'mysterious' or as 'teacher's party trick' (i.e. as something that they cannot expect to explain, and do not need to explain).

The teacher also has to be wary of the possibility that pupils may partly accept the new framework, but may distort it to enable them to retain most of their previous thinking. For example, Nussbaum and Novick suggest that pupils who think the earth is flat, presented with evidence which points to a round earth, may think in terms of the earth as a flat circular disc, thus retaining their flat model but incorporating something of the new idea of roundness. The appropriateness of the teacher's language, and the scope of the evidence presented to pupils, may both affect the likelihood of such partial learning. This is consistent with the idea put forward by Posner and colleagues (1982) who suggest that such a sequence of teaching will only work if the new framework is readily understandable and clearly explained, and if it is not too far removed from what the pupils already know.

Hashweh (1986) adds some further suggestions to improve this basic teaching tactic. He suggests that we should take care to:

- ensure that the pupils' original ideas are never treated as wrong, but merely as ideas of limited application – decent ideas built perhaps on limited evidence, or misperceptions, or special cases
- show that the new ideas based on formal science works where their ideas worked

- show that the new ideas work where their ideas did not
- point out the differences between these situations

Watts and Bentley (1987) also argue that this active role for the pupil makes considerable demands on them in that they are being expected to reveal their thinking and to be open minded enough to change that thinking. This is only likely to happen in a supportive classroom environment where the teacher takes care to accept pupils' ideas seriously and is also unwilling to allow pupils to ridicule one another's thinking.

There are two main reasons for discussing pupils' alternative frameworks and the associated constructivist view of learning. First, they provide us with powerful tactics for differentiating teaching for all pupils (e.g. by class-based brainstorming of explanations and subsequent planning of class practical work to investigate at least some of them). Secondly, they provide ideas for attending to the science-related learning difficulties which might be faced by some pupils with special needs (e.g. by individual interviews about instances and individualised treatment of their own ideas on a one-to-one basis). However, Selley (1981) points out that the constructivist view of learning science is also consistent with the vision of science itself as a system of models which describe how the world might be, rather than a set of statements about how it actually is. In this view, the models created by scientists derive their validity not from their accuracy in describing the real world, but from the accuracy of any predictions which might be based upon them. To ask if gravity really exists is to ask the wrong question; the right question is whether the concept of gravity and its associated detail such as the inverse square law, enables us to make accurate predictions of planetary motion, tides, etc. If it does then gravity is a good model which is worth preserving in our scientific toolbag. A further reason for adopting a constructivist approach to science teaching is therefore that it enables us to help pupils towards a more sophisticated understanding of the nature of science.

Tactics related to differences in pupils' understanding of basic concepts

The tactics based on APU, on Gagné's theory, and on the constructivist model of learning, all have a wide range of application in science. They can be expected to help us to focus teaching on individual pupils' needs across most of the content of the science syllabus. They help us to be more sensitive to the needs of able pupils, as well as to those of pupils with learning difficulties. However, there are other sources of insight into ways of dealing with pupils who have difficulties with very basic concepts. These deserve brief attention as they may be particularly valuable in helping the most disadvantaged of the pupils whom we are likely to meet in secondary schools. Some of these tactics are fairly much a matter of commonsense. Once we have been sensitised to the fact that pupils may have difficulties with quite basic things like concepts related to space and time, we can use our routine experience as teachers to devise simple instructional tactics which are very likely to help. Raban and Postlethwaite (1988) describe several tactics of this kind. Though it is impossible, in a book of this size, to describe many such tactics in sufficient detail to enable teachers to make direct use of them, some examples are included below – partly because they may be useful in their own right, and partly because they indicate the *kind* of thing which is called for.

For teachers looking for further guidance, it is helpful to note that Adey and his colleagues (1989a) have gone beyond common sense and have used insights from Piaget's work and from that of Feuerstein (see later in this chapter) to develop an extensive, theoretically grounded range of ideas covering many important aspects of thinking related to science. These have been the topic of systematic evaluation, and have been shown to be helpful to pupils (Adey and Shayer, 1990).

Space

Some pupils (like Lucy who was mentioned in Chapter 1) have difficulty with science, partly because they are unsure about concepts that are concerned with position in space. If the notions of 'left' and 'right' are insecure, what hope does the child have of understanding the discussion of factors affecting the force on a wire in the catapult field experiment? If 'towards' is a concept without meaning, how can children appreciate explanations of electroplating phrased in terms of charged particles moving towards oppositely charged electrodes? If the concept 'below' has little meaning for the pupil, how can they understand the geological significance of the fact that older fossils are below newer ones in a cliff face? This same conceptual problem may also prevent a pupil from following our explanation when we say that copper is below magnesium in the reactivity series, or that an interesting result can be found two lines below the top in a table. If we recognise that learning problems in these areas might go back as far as problems with these basic spatial concepts we will also recognise the need to develop tactics to help pupils understand them.

Such tactics can often take the form of simple games on which pupils might work in pairs or small groups. For example, one pupil can be given a photograph of objects (e.g. standard laboratory equipment) in a simple arrangement. That pupil then gives instructions to the other pupil to arrange the same real items to match the photograph. The pupils then compare the arrangement with the photograph and discuss any discrepancies. In such discussion the teacher ensures that the pupils are using spatial terms in appropriate ways. At first the arrangements should be simple so that a very few instructions will suffice; later, more complex arrangements might be used. At this stage the first pupil would be encouraged to write down the instructions so that they can still be checked at the end. Where writing is a problem, the first pupil might be given a worksheet on which the instructions are given in a multiple choice format (e.g. the beaker is above/below/to the left of/to the right of the tripod). All the pupil then needs to do is to underline the instruction that she thinks is correct as she gives it to her partner.

In a follow-up task, pupils might be given copies of a simple street map. The first pupil has a map

on which the buildings are named or numbered; the other pupil has a map on which they are unlabelled or labelled by letter only. The pupils agree on a starting point. The first pupil then issues instructions to the other to guide them to another building. The second pupil follows these instructions on their own map. At the end of the sequence of instructions they compare notes and discuss any discrepancies in the planned and executed journeys. Again, first attempts should be limited to short sequences of instruction. Later on pupils can try more complex journeys which may again need writing down in order that the subsequent discussion can take place. The map task is much more complex than the task of arranging apparatus as it involves changes in frame of reference as the pupils imagine themselves moving around the space defined by the map.

Computer-based versions of these games can obviously be valuable, not least because they offer opportunities for immediate feedback to the pupil without the teacher's continuous presence. One readily-available program which could be used in this way is LOGO. As a pupil issues LOGO instructions to turn right, turn left, etc. a 'turtle' can be seen to turn in that direction. 'Real world' motor-driven turtles are better here than on-screen turtles for there can clearly be a problem for the pupil in entering the frame of reference of an object on a vertical screen in order to anticipate what effect the instruction 'turn right' will produce. The fact that such an instruction would result in a turtle that was moving horizontally across the screen turning to move up or down the screen world hardly help a pupil to untangle notions of right and left from those of up and down!

It is interesting that the process of checking intended and achieved outcomes in such games can also provide opportunities for the teacher and pupils to discuss strategies for systematic, nonimpulsive and precise observation (Raban and Postlethwaite, 1988, pp. 14–15). In doing so, further areas of potential weakness to which I drew attention earlier in this chapter for the pupils can be addressed. In all of the work described in this section, the discussion that takes place between pupils and teacher is crucial. It is here that pupils attention is drawn explicitly to the spatial concepts with which we are concerned, and to the fact that they have been able to handle these successfully. It is therefore through such discussion that pupils' competence and confidence in working with spatial relationships grows.

Time

Difficulties with concepts related to time can cause significant problems for pupils. Some science lessons make direct use of time (e.g. in discussion about rates of reaction, or of speed and acceleration, or of human reaction times and the consequences for road safety, or of the geological development of the earth) and the different units and vastly different time scales involved here may not be very meaningful to some pupils. Some lessons require an understanding of time in more subtle ways: for example, clarity about the temporal sequence in which something happens is essential to consideration of possible causes for the effects seen. Also, in all lessons, pupils' difficulties in managing their time within the problem solving process (see Chapter 2) could well relate to difficulties that they have with the concept of time itself if, for example, they have no real feel for how much time is available to them when the teacher says they have 10 minutes for a task.

To attempt to remedy these problems it may be helpful to establish basic concepts such as 'before' and 'after' by asking pupils to sequence pictures of processes which are relevant to science and which are presented to them in a random order. These may be sequences of everyday events with a science content (such as ice melting to form a puddle and the puddle evaporating), or sequences of steps in an already familiar experiment. Sequencing tasks of this kind can be used on material involving a wide range of time intervals up to a few weeks or even months. The more familiar the context, the longer the time intervals that pupils may, initially, be able to handle. For example, sequencing pictures of familiar seasonal change taking place throughout a year might well be a realistic task, whereas sequences of a relatively unfamiliar laboratory process may need to

be confined to steps which take place within the length of a single school lesson if they are to be accessible to the pupils. As in the case of work on spatial concepts, activities such as these sequencing tasks should be followed up by discussion in which pupils are asked to make explicit the reasons for the sequence they have chosen and to discuss and evaluate other sequences that may have been chosen by peers. The teacher's role in such discussion is to ensure that notions such as 'before' and 'after' are used with understanding.

To give pupils a sense of the magnitude of common units of time, a variety of activities can be used. It is helpful to begin with work on time intervals which are meaningful to pupils in terms of day-to-day life. Short time intervals – say in the range 10 to 30 seconds – can be worked on by asking pupils to estimate the length of short events and then to measure the time with a stopwatch. Longer intervals of up to one hour can be handled by reference to an analogue clock face. For example, pupils can compare the sector of the clock face equivalent to 15 minutes to the whole 1 hour circle (using cut out 15 minute sectors if necessary); pupils can compare the sector equivalent to 5 minutes to that for 15 minutes, and so on. In these ways a basic understanding of common time intervals and their relationships can be reinforced. (It is interesting to speculate that exclusive use of digital clocks could well contribute to some pupils' lack of 'feel' for the length of time intervals in the range 5 minutes to 60 minutes.) Discussion of the equivalence of different units may also be helpful at this stage. For example, pupils may be asked to say whether 20 seconds is shorter, longer or the same as 1 minute, or whether 11 hours is longer or shorter than a day. (This is not trivial in that common usage may encourage children to think of a day as the hours of daylight which may well be less than 11 hours!) Computer programs, and hardware such as the Unilab computer interface, can be of particular use here, partly because some of them make it easy to present such work in a games format, but more especially because they provide immediate feedback to the pupil.

For very short time intervals, extended use of the tickertimer as a clock can be very helpful.

For most pupils the time-measuring role of this equipment is not problematic and little difficulty is caused by moving quickly from its first introduction to its role in analysing speed. However, for pupils who have difficulties with the notion of time, the fairly direct way in which the timer represents short time intervals can provide a real stimulus for understanding that very short-lived events do nevertheless take time. For example, pupils can measure the time for which one hand is in motion during a handclap simply by attaching tickertape to the moving hand and then counting the number of spaces between dots.

Very long time intervals may best be handled by reference to time lines which enable the pupil to make sense of abstract relationships such as before and after, in terms of more concrete relationships of left and right. The relative nature of time terms can also be illustrated. For example, by plotting dates on a time line drawn on a scale of, say, 1 cm = 10 years pupils can be helped to recognise that, in 1900, 1950 was in the future. This can be very helpful in any discussion of the history of science (e.g. by helping pupils to realise things that were not known at the time a particular idea was being developed, but which are now taken for granted).

Tactics related to differences in pupils' reading ability

Differences in pupils' ability to read text are best classified as educational differences because they reflect differences in what pupils can already *do*. This is just as important an element of prior learning as what they already know and understand. As science teachers, we should clearly share the task of remediating reading difficulties if at all possible. This is partly because all teachers have a general responsibility for helping pupils to acquire such an important basic skill, but also because there are characteristics of reading in science which, to some extent, set it apart from reading generally.

The mathematical language of some science, and the use of chemical shorthand serve as two examples of aspects of scientific writing where the pupil has to read every symbol in order to decode the text accurately. Word-by-word, and especially symbol-by-symbol reading is not a skill which a pupil needs to develop to read many kinds of book – particularly to read novels for pleasure. The English or Special Needs teacher, working to support pupils' general reading, will help pupils to develop the skill of reading fluently. The teacher may even encourage pupils to move away from word-by-word reading in order to help them to become involved in the general flow of a story and to begin to appreciate the enjoyment that reading can provide. Science teachers should, of course, try to reinforce this vital aspect of reading ability, but we also have an important role in encouraging pupils to develop the word-by-word, and symbol-by-symbol reading skills which are complementary to fluency, and so necessary to successful reading in our subject area. We are also well placed to help pupils recognise when each type of reading is appropriate.

Guidance on how we can attend to reading difficulties can be drawn from a wide range of sources. These include the use of readability scores and reading age tests to match texts to pupils, the use of comprehension tests and cloze tests (see below) to check the matches that have been made to that better judgements can be made in the future, and the use of carefully structured reading tasks that focus pupils' attention on particular outcomes for their reading. These techniques can be viewed as remedial strategies if the main aim is to encourage better reading by ensuring success on well-chosen and well-structured reading tasks. However, they can also be viewed as circumvention strategies if the teacher sees them only as methods of getting particular content across through the medium of text despite pupils' weaknesses in reading. The difference will depend on whether, in talking to the pupil about the work, the teacher stresses the reading skills that were in use or the content that was being read. (Discussion of the reading skills would include: talking about any words pupils found difficult; asking whether they were able to find clues in the text that helped them sort out what difficult words or sections might mean; encouraging them to use any diagrams etc. to support their understanding; directing their attention to the use of the index to help solve difficulties . . .) Even if our focus is fairly heavily on the content, it is interesting that by giving *some* attention to these aspects of reading, we can support the more specialist remedial reading help that a pupil may be receiving elsewhere, and begin to meet the aim of helping the pupil to develop skills for reading science that I mentioned above.

What, then, is available as guidance on the match of reading to pupils, and on the design of reading tasks, that will enable us to help our pupils to learn science, and to learn about reading science? Harrison (1980) describes a range of *readability formulae* which enable teachers to make an estimate of the difficulty which a given text is likely to present to pupils before actually offering the text to the pupil. Most of these formulae give a result which can be interpreted as the age that a reader of average ability would have to have in order to be likely to be able to cope with the text with the support of the teacher. The *SMOG formula* (which is described in Appendix 3 and is very simple to apply) is standardised differently, and can be interpreted as giving the age for unsupported use of the text. It is important to recognise that such formulae are not precise indicators of the difficulty of a text and should perhaps be regarded as indicating a range of about three years over which the text might be effective (e.g. a readability score of 12 might be seen as justifying use of a text, in class, with 11–13-year old average readers).

Readability formulae tend to concentrate on grammatical factors such as the proportion of long words and the length of sentences in a piece of writing. However, long words are not always difficult words – especially in science texts. For example, it is unlikely that pupils who are reading about temperature measurement in the context of lessons where thermometers are in use and are frequently referred to in conversation, would find the word 'thermometer' difficult to read. Its frequent appearance in a piece of text could, however, inflate the readability score for that text. In contrast, several factors which would not contribute to the scores returned by most readability formulae could nevertheless make text more difficult to read. Such factors might include the size and style of the font used, the layout of text on the page (e.g. the line spacing and even the point in the sentence at which the line breaks occur), the relationship between text and photographs or drawings, the frequency of use of short but unusual words, the unfamiliar use of common words (e.g. the unusual use of the word 'returned' in the previous sentence), the order of ideas in a sentence, and the complexity of the ideas themselves. Perera (1980, 1986) discusses many of these factors at length. It follows that readability formulae can only be used as a guide, but as they focus attention on factors that may not be easy to judge by inspection, they remain useful guides.

Readability formulae, together with the insights provided by Perera, can help us to choose appropriate text for the pupils we are to teach. They can also help us to produce more appropriate written materials (such as worksheets, revision notes, and comprehension exercises) for our pupils' use. See Raban and Postlethwaite (1988) for further details.

Reading-age tests can be applied to pupils to establish whether they are average readers (reading age equal to chronological age) or not (reading age above, or below chronological age). Such tests are quite a common element in special needs department record keeping and can give some confirmatory evidence on the extent of an individual's reading difficulties. A useful review of such tests is provided by Vincent and colleagues (1983). One might imagine that the use of readability scores and reading age would enable us to make a better match between text and pupil than the use of readability scores and chronological age. Up to a point this is true. There are, however, dangers in assuming that a text with a readability score of 12 will necessarily suit a 16-year-old poor reader with a reading age of 12 – the style and content of the text may well make it quite unacceptable to the older pupil whose background knowledge and interests are unlikely to match those of the 12-year olds for whom the text was originally intended. The teacher will therefore need to make a subjective judgement about these issues as well as using the tests as a guide.

Use of readability formulae and reading-age tests, together with assessments of the other factors mentioned above, can help the teacher to make judgements about the suitability of a text for an intended purpose in advance of its actual use. These judgements can be checked after use of the text by means of cloze tests or comprehension tests. If pupils score 90 per cent or more on a comprehension test based on a text, it is safe to assume that the text can be used independently of the teacher by those pupils; if they score 75 per cent the text is suitable for use with the support of the teacher. Cloze tests are those in which a piece of text is modified by deletion of every fifth word. Pupils are then asked to read the text and fill the gaps. Marks are awarded only for words which are identical to those used by the author. Under this regime, scores of 60 per cent indicate that the text is suitable for unsupported use; scores of 40–45 per cent show that it can be used with the support of the teacher.

Support for poor readers is not limited to the selection of texts which match their abilities and interests. Pupils can be helped to gain information from quite a wide range of texts if they are set carefully designed reading tasks which structure their work with the text. It can, for example, be helpful if any reading which pupils do on their own is preceded by discussion in class, and followed by writing. It can be even more helpful if their reading is itself a group-based, interactive process. An excellent set of ideas for helping pupils to work with text in this way are the Directed Activities Related to Text (DARTs) developed by Lunzer and Gardner (1984) and described in the context of science teaching by Davies and Greene (1984). These DARTs activities can be divided into three groups: text reconstruction, text analysis and text representation. Some examples of DARTs activities are included in the material presented in Appendix 2.

Text reconstruction activities are those in which pupils are presented with text which has been modified in some way. The pupils' task, in small groups, is to read the modified text and work together to reconstruct something which has the same meaning as the original. For example, words can be omitted from the original text and pupils have then to reconstruct the whole thing, or labels can be omitted from diagrams and pupils have to fill them in from the text, or an incomplete diagram is offered and pupils have to complete it from information in the text, or pupils have to annotate a diagram from such information. Although the exercise of filling in missing words in the text sounds similar to the cloze tests described above, it actually differs from it in several important ways. First, its purpose is to encourage learning, not to test it. Secondly, in the DARTs exercise words are not omitted at regular intervals. Instead, the omissions are carefully chosen to focus pupils' attention on the point of the lesson. If we were trying to improve pupils' understanding of the principles of experiment design we might modify a text describing a particular investigation, by leaving out words which relate to the identification of relevant variables, or to the criteria for choice of apparatus, or to the method of control of variables. If we were interested in the concepts being developed by the same piece of text we might focus attention on them by leaving out only words which relate to these concepts. Thirdly, pupils are not required to find the exact word(s) used by the original author. The important thing is their reconstruction of the sense of the piece. Further important aspects of the preparation of text for this completion exercise are that pupils should be given a 'lead in' of several lines in which no omissions are made so that they can get some sense of what the text is about, and that we should not delete all references to an idea from the prepared text. To do so would force pupils into a guessing game. Similar guidelines apply to the preparation of diagrams for reconstruction exercises. What we want to encourage in each case is discussion about the missing elements based on what the pupils have read earlier in the passage, or later. As well as focusing their attention on the ideas with which we are concerned, this develops their ability to tease out meaning from text based on the context which precedes and follows a section with which they may be having difficulty.

A different kind of text reconstruction is that in which a piece of text is shortened by omitting the final section. Pupils then have to predict how the piece ended, basing their views on what they have read and justifying them to one another in the group and, perhaps through subsequent writing, to the teacher. This task can be extended by breaking a piece of text into a series of sections. Pupils read (or listen to) just the first section, the teacher then asks a question aimed at helping pupils to predict the next step. Pupils discuss this in groups then report back briefly to the class. The teacher then reads the next section and discusses the various predictions in relation to the actual text. The teacher then asks a new question which prompts the pupils to consider the next stage in the argument. The process is continued until the text is complete. This exercise works best where there is a strong line of development in the text, e.g. in the case of a description of a process.

A somewhat similar task is that of sequencing. Here the teacher gives pupils a whole text which has been broken into steps and each step has been written on a separate card. The cards are shuffled and the pupils have to put the text back into sequence. This works very well with experiment instructions or other text in which there is a strong sense of sequence. It ensures that pupils read and think about every step before starting their practical work. Pupils' attention can easily be drawn to safety points, for example by writing them on differently coloured cards. This activity does not work at all with descriptive text which can be presented in practically any order. If possible, the text should not contain words which give away the sequence directly (e.g. 'first', 'secondly', 'finally' etc.). Pupils should have to reconstruct the order from an understanding of the points made by the text, not simply from a recognition of these direct clues.

Text analysis activities make use of unmodified text and include the tasks of underlining, segmenting and labelling. In the underlining activity, pupils are asked to underline words or phrases which serve a particular function in the text. For example, pupils might be asked to underline all the examples of expansion in a passage on heat. This can be extended to the task of underlining advantageous examples in one colour and troublesome examples in another. Two-colour underlining can also be used to identify different kinds of information in a passage. For example pupils could be asked to underline the parts of a flower in one colour and the function of these parts in another. The physical difficulty of writing on text books can be overcome in a variety of ways. In some circumstances photocopies of the text could be used, or pupils could do their underlining on acetate sheets, or could use paperclips to attach slips of paper to the page and write the key word on the paper. Segmenting and labelling activities can often be done as two parts of one activity. In the segmenting activity pupils are asked to break the text into sections which stand as units of information in some way; in labelling activities they attach labels to these segments. These labels, which are usually provided by the teacher, can either summarise the section, or describe the function which it is performing (e.g. describes a model; criticises a conclusion, etc.).

Text representation activities ask the pupils to present the information in the text in some other format. They could, for example, be asked to draw up a table, or an annotated diagram, or flow chart. The amount of support offered (e.g. whether column headings for a table are provided or not) can be varied according to pupils' overall ability in the subject.

Pupil discussion, during the lesson, about the text and the task which is based upon it, is a crucial aspect of all of these DARTs activities. The activities can often be followed up by a writing task. For example, pupils might take away with them the labels produced during a text labelling exercise and use them as a guide to re-write the main ideas of the text in their own words. This offers more support to the pupil than a simple request to 'Write it up at home' but it avoids the unproductive activity of direct copying of the text book.

As well as helping poor readers to learn from the usual range of school text books, these techniques can help able pupils who are good readers to cope with very demanding material so can serve as useful components of text-based enrichment tasks.

Some theoretical justification for DARTs can be found in the list of characteristics of pupils with learning difficulties which can be derived from information processing models. These were listed in Chapter 2. For example, pupils working with DARTs have very well-structured tasks to do which focus their attention on the particular issue which the teacher wishes to address. They are therefore helped to define exactly what they are meant to be concentrating on – something which appears to present many pupils with difficulty. Similarly, the group-based discussion which is a feature of DARTs activities helps pupils to make the ideas their own, encourages them to link the new ideas to their own previous thinking and therefore supports them in remembering the new material – something, again, which such pupils tend to find difficult. This gives us a basis for believing that DARTs may well prove to be effective. In an annotated bibliography to their book, Davies and Greene (1984) draw attention to several empirical studies which have confirmed this effectiveness.

Earlier in this section we described readability tests and DARTs activities as having both remedial and circumvention aspects. In some circumstances pupils' reading difficulties may be so great that these tactics do not work in either aspect of their role. The science teacher may not feel competent (or, more likely, may not have the time) to use more basic remedial procedures. In such circumstances pure circumvention tactics may be required. These could include reading text or worksheets on to audiotape so that the pupil can listen to the material instead of reading it. Videotaped readings including close-ups of pictures or other visual support for the material may be even more accessible. Some computer software is becoming available which allows the computer to 'speak' the text which is being displayed on the screen. It is possible for pupils to record their verbal responses to such programs directly in the computer memory so that their work can be made

available to the teacher even if their writing is also a handicap to communication. Such tactics clearly require careful preparation by the science teacher. Non-teaching assistants may be available in the science class to read material to the pupil, but again their effectiveness is limited unless the science teacher spends time explaining to them the aims of the lesson and the key points which are to be tackled through the reading.

Tactics related to differences in pupils' grasp of numeracy

Cockcroft (DES, 1982) drew sharp attention to the fact that pupils differ considerably from one another in their ability to work with mathematical concepts and techniques when he referred to the 'seven year difference in achieving an understanding of place value which is sufficient to write down the number which is 1 more than 6399'. A major element in attending to this aspect of educational differences is that of language. As Cockcroft points out 'mathematics provides a means of communication which is powerful concise and unambiguous'. Unfortunately, when teacher and pupil try to use this language, communication is not always the result. There are several aspects of this.

1 Different teachers often use different terms to say the same thing: one teacher may say 'multiply', another 'times'; one teacher may say 'raised to the power 3', another may say 'cubed'. The variety in our language can nicely be demonstrated by getting colleagues to read out an expression such as $4.01 \times (6y + 9)^3$. Several versions will almost certainly be provided: 'four point oh one'; 'four decimal zero one'; 'to the power three'; 'cubed'; 'open brackets, six y plus nine, close brackets'; 'six times y add nine all in brackets', etc. Such variety presents no difficulties for pupils who are confident in mathematics. Indeed, as they will undoubtedly meet all these versions in discussions which have a mathematical element, one could argue that to meet it in school is an important aspect of their

mathematical education. However, for the pupil who has difficulty with mathematics, such variety is just additional noise which obscures the message. One tactic for helping such pupils is therefore to establish a common language amongst the teachers in a school who make use of mathematics in their teaching. Special needs staff should, of course, be included in this range of staff.

2 The language of mathematics may not be un-ambiguous to the pupil. It often overlaps with common language and the pupil may make inappropriate connections between the two. Perhaps when new technical terms such as 'area' are introduced, or when we first return to a topic that uses them, we should ask, 'What does the word "area" mean to you?' We would then be in a position to make the mathematical use of the term explicit, and to add meaning to it by drawing links with the individual pupil's common usage and indicating where the two usages diverge.

3 An analysis of teachers' non-technical language in class has revealed that we tend to use more complex sentence structures when discussing mathematics than when discussing other subject content (Howarth, 1985). This can obviously present pupils with difficulties in understanding if their own language ability is weak or if they are struggling with the mathematical ideas which are embedded in this more complex teacher talk. Experienced teachers may find that knowing of this risk is enough to enable them to avoid it; beginning teachers may find it helpful to plan the language in which they will discuss the mathematical aspects of their lessons more fully.

4 Kerslake (1982) points out that to understand and act upon the precise language of math-ematical symbols, pupils have to decode them into normal language that can guide their action. $3x$ only has meaning if it is decoded into a statement such as 'whatever value x has, $3x$ has three times that value'. We should give pupils practice in coding and decoding of this kind. In particular, we should note that there are often different ways of verbalising symbols and that sometimes one of these will lead to progress whereas others may lead to dead ends. For example, 12/2 can be verbalised as 'How many twos are there in twelve?', and as 'What would each person get if twelve was divided between two people?'. Only the first of these is likely to help a pupil faced with calculating the value of $12/\frac{1}{2}$. We should therefore help pupils to be aware of the range of ways of verbalising for-mulae and to recognise the value of trying out different ways as steps in trying to solve a prob-lem. This does not contradict the need for con-sistency. The variation being advocated here is useful variation; 'four point oh one' and 'four decimal zero one' are not in any way helpful variations.

5 We may need to arrange for a fuller exchange of mathematical language with our pupils. Much of the language which they use to deal with problems which have a mathematical element is usually hidden from us. We see only the re-sults of their work; the all important language which led to these results is often private to the pupil. Asking pupils to work in groups on mathematical problems so that they share the language of solution with one another is one powerful tool which can be expected to improve pupils' fluency in language associated with mathematics. The group situation can also legitimate the trial of partially formed ideas: 'I don't know whether this will work but why don't we try . . .' and the testing of solutions against general principles: 'No, that can't be right. Surely it's bound to be bigger than the thing we started with . . .' Of course, if we can join in these group discussions we will be able to sug-gest ways of talking though the problem and will be able to listen to pupils with the purpose of diagnosis of their difficulties in mind. One part of our contribution to discussion can be to draw attention to errors made by the pupils in ways that encourage them to continue the de-bate, rather than simply accept that they have failed. Bishop has drawn attention to some helpful tactics of this kind such as showing that their approach would lead to a silly answer that they can recognise is wrong, or drawing atten-tion to a specific step with a comment such as,

'Haven't you forgotten the decimal point here?' (see Kerslake, 1982, for further details).

Alongside this more explicit attention to the role of pupils' language in working with mathematics, we may, as teachers, profitably share more of our own mathematical language with pupils. Our presentation of mathematical solutions to pupils is often that of a polished performance where we move linearly to the solution. It may well be helpful to pupils if we were sometimes to reveal the whole of the process: the possible alternative starting points; our reasons for choosing one rather than another to begin with; how we sense a dead end; what we do when we reach a dead end; how we might work back from the solution if we get stuck.

Once this more open attention to the mathematical language of both the teacher and the pupils has been established as part of lessons where maths has an important role, it may be realistic to ask pupils to reveal something of their private mathematical language in their written work. We could, for example, ask them to write about their problem-solving at the end of a set of mathematical questions? Questions such as the following might encourage pupils to write things that will help us to help them in the development of their mathematical skills: 'What did you find interesting about these questions? What did . . . mean to you? Did you get stuck anywhere? What did you try to get yourself "unstuck"? How did you check that your answers were reasonable? What still puzzles you?' We should, however, be alert to the possibility that able pupils might find this writing tedious as they do not need the support that can come from this reflection and from the teacher's help which can be based upon it.

These tactics are all essentially remedial tactics. We should note, however, that the calculator can serve as a useful tool for the circumvention of some mathematical difficulties – particularly those awkward computational problems that accompany the processing of real experimental data where numbers rarely come out in ways that simplify the arithmetic. We should be aware that some pupils will need help in entering data and operators into calculators, and in interpreting results – especially where the calculator produces a large number of decimal places. We should also, where possible, encourage pupils to make rough estimates of answers so that they can check their calculator work. If we do plan to use calculators, it is reassuring that the Cockcroft Report (DES, 1982) argued that their use had no adverse effect on basic computational skills.

Spreadsheets have similar functions as tools for circumventing computational difficulties. For example pupils working with Newton's Second Law could be offered a spreadsheet in which sections permit the calculation of the value of F, m or a, given the other two variables. However, combined with thoughtful teaching, such spreadsheets can have a more significant value. They can encourage pupils to explore relationships, e.g. to see that the mathematical law leads one to expect that, for constant F, as m increases, a decreases. This can be checked against experience and a feel for the implications of the law can be built up. Also, confidence gained through using a spreadsheet to get answers to problems on $F = ma$ might encourage pupils to work with a teacher to explore the relationships between the three variables (e.g. that the value of F that you get is m times a, or that the value of a is F/m). These concrete examples might then be used by the teacher to lead the pupil on to appreciation of the processes involved in changing the subject of equations.

Educational differences – summary

In general, the tactics discussed above are remedial tactics in that we expect pupils' understanding to change as a result of what we do with them. This is to be expected in that the whole notion of an education system presupposes a belief that educational differences are unstable, that increased understanding is to be valued and that change towards this condition lies, at least in some measure, within the teacher's control. We should not, however, overlook the fact that the sequencing of learning might make it necessary to devise circumvention tactics that enable a pupil to learn X without first mastering Y which is a necessary step in learning X but also a source of difficulty for the pupil. For example, we may wish pupils to test the idea that the current is the same all round a simple series circuit. To do this convincingly the pupil may need to read an ammeter to a precision that would imply accurate estimation of readings that lie between the scale divisions of an analogue instrument, and we might know that some of our pupils have great difficulty with this. Such skill in scale reading is clearly something which we would want to encourage, but we might recognise that to put emphasis on this skill will deflect the attention of these pupils from the testing of the concept of constant current. We might therefore decide to adopt the circumvention tactic of using a digital ammeter, or of tweaking the experiment so that current readings lie exactly on scale divisions, so that these pupils can appreciate the point about current flow in spite of their continuing difficulty over precise scale interpolation. This would seem to be a very sensible decision as long as we recognise what we are doing, and as long as we find other opportunities (perhaps in the same few lessons, though perhaps much later) to help the pupil develop the scale reading skill. Circumvention tactics related to reading or numeracy may also have a place where the extent of a pupil's problem is such that it is impracticable for the science teacher to persist with attempts at remediation. We should however recognise that this leaves the pupil without valuable skills and should, at very least, ensure that someone is addressing these with the pupil. The general point, therefore, is that tactics for the circumvention of educational differences may be valuable to the science teacher in some situations, but that generally our long-term aim should be to find ways of remediating pupils' educational difficulties if this is at all possible.

TACTICS RELATED TO PSYCHOLOGICAL DIFFERENCES

Tactics related to differences in pupils' intelligence (structure of intellect)

At the beginning of this chapter, I pointed out that the work on intelligence that I quoted in Chapter 2 was likely to have greater impact on our attitudes to pupils, than on the specific tactics which we use to teach them. However, some work on Guilford's multifactorial model of intelligence has generated specific teaching tactics and a possible implication of these for the science teacher will be discussed briefly below.

Through the Structure of Intellect (SOI) Institute in California, test materials are available that help to diagnose pupils' strengths and weaknesses in terms of Guilford's Structure of Intellect Model. In addition, remedial exercises have been produced which are designed to develop those areas in which a given pupil is weak. Very briefly, Guilford's model proposes that intelligence can be thought of as a three dimensional matrix. Different 'operations' on one dimension act on different 'content' on another to produce different 'products' on a third. Examples of operations are memory (which is self-explanatory) and divergent production (the ability to find a range of solutions to problems which do not have a unique solution). Examples of content are symbolic content (letters, numbers, notations) and semantic content (the meanings of words). Products include units (single blocks of information) and classes (well-defined groups). Thus 'divergent production of symbolic classes' might be assessed by the ability to find many different ways of forming the numbers 2,3,4,7,9,11,12 into two groups (even/odd; multiples of three/not multiples of three; prime/not prime; squares of integers/not squares of integers . . .). A pupil may be generally weak on the operation 'divergent production'. He or she may, on the other hand, be relatively strong on most aspects of semantic content and on most aspects of the product 'classes'. Remedial exercises for such a pupil would stress divergent production of semantic classes – building on the pupils' strength with semantic classes to give scope for the development of the divergent production operation.

Evaluations of the materials, which were conducted independently but published through the SOI lnstitute, suggest that the remedial exercises can improve performance on the relevant SOI tests, and also offer some suggestion that performance in related areas of the school curriculum can be improved through their use. The criticisms that have been levelled at Guilford's model in general, do suggest that caution may be needed in interpreting these results, but they do seem to offer some indication that the procedure can be valuable.

Of course, to work directly on the different factors of intelligence identified in Guilford's model it would be necessary to use the SOI materials and therefore to acquire them through the SOI lnstitute. However, it may be possible to gain inspiration from the idea that one should look at the pupils' profile of test scores to identify areas in which performance is weak and then work to develop these in the context of areas where performance is relatively strong. In the science teaching context one might notice a pupils' difficulties in mathematical reasoning and her strength in work on biology and seek to develop mathematical skills with reference to biological material; alternatively a pupil who has difficulty with experimental design but is good at electricity might be provided with design challenges which are based in the context of electricity.

Tactics related to motivation

In Chapter 2, I referred to the fact that there are many different models of human motivation and argued that links between individuals' motivation and their achievements are complex. This certainly implies that motivating pupils in a class may be a far more subtle matter than simply that of finding interesting ways of presenting a given topic to them. This may, in turn, explain why our very best attempts to teach in an interesting fashion are sometimes met with indifference or even with negative reactions from some pupils. Our consequent feelings of anger ('After all I've done to prepare this lesson and provide such interesting activities, all you can do is mess about . . !') may be understandable, but should perhaps be a spur to a closer investigation of the issue of motivation, rather than a reason for giving up on a class or an individual.

Maslow's model of motivation states, for example, that there is a hierarchy of basic needs:

- needs to fulfil one's own potential
- needs for self-esteem (recognition from others and personal feelings of competence)
- needs for affiliation and affection
- needs for physical and psychological safety
- physiological needs (needs for food, warmth, etc.)

Alongside these basic needs, there is a hierarchy of cognitive needs (including the need to acquire knowledge and understanding, and the need to analyse and organise such knowledge). Satisfying the cognitive needs plays a part in satisfying the basic needs – e.g. the child needs information in order to contribute to his or her own safety. In Maslow's view, a person will devote their energies mainly to meeting the lowest need in the basic needs hierarchy which, for them, has not yet been met to a satisfactory degree. It is therefore clear that a teacher working with a hungry, or insecure, or unloved child is likely to get little return from a really interesting presentation of work on, say, respiration. Some attempts will have to be made to help such pupil fulfil their more fundamental basic needs if they are to begin to engage with the knowledge-related goals which we are setting up for them.

Maslow's work implies that there will be limits to what an individual teacher can achieve in this respect, especially where needs which still have to be met are very low in the basic needs hierarchy. However, it also suggests that the teacher is not powerless. Well-established routines in school and in class might contribute to a pupil's sense of psychological security; cooperative work amongst pupils might encourage a sense of affiliation; a dogged determination on the part of the teacher to signal approval of pupils as individuals even when their work or behaviour requires (and receives) a critical response might convey a sense of affection; supportive feedback on pupils' work, display of work in the classroom, the production of work for audiences other than that of the teacher, and a determination on the part of the teacher to respond positively to a pupil's ideas and to discourage dismissive responses from other pupils, might all offer pupils a sense of recognition and self-esteem. These more general aspects of the affective environment in which we teach will not remove the need to find interesting ways of putting across the ideas of respiration, but they may well help to guarantee that energy devoted to the design of such teaching methods will not be wasted.

In Chapter 2, I also mentioned McClelland's idea of achievement motivation – motivation rooted in the pupil's need to achieve (nAch). Although the relationships between nAch and attainment have not been demonstrated with consistency (McClelland, 1972) and are undoubtedly complex, it seems that there might be value in trying to raise nAch levels on the part of individuals for which this is low. In one study, McClelland and Winter (1969) devised a programme of training designed to increase nAch and subsequent performance. This involved such things as discussion of, and involvement in, the styles of thinking of people with high nAch, consideration of the benefits of risk-taking and of delayed rewards, consideration of the participant's own self-image and career goals, and training in how to assess one's own progress towards such goals. de Charms

and colleagues (1969) trained teachers to introduce nAch training of this kind to their own pupils and demonstrated that when teachers worked with pupils on this approach at appropriate times throughout a year, significant effects on school performance were produced. One might therefore be encouraged to try building work of this kind into one's tutorial work with pupils, if not into one's science teaching.

The points discussed above represent a remedial approach to pupils with low nAch. If, as a result of the lack of clarity in the evaluations of attempts to change nAch, we prefer to regard it as a relatively stable pupil characteristic, we must look for a way of circumventing the effects of low nAch scores. A different model, that of 'motivation for achievement', may offer a way forward for the teacher. Weiner (1976) points out that a pupil's overall motivation to engage in an achievement-oriented task (M) is related to the pupil's nAch, but also to the pupil's expectation of the probability of success in the task (P) and to the pupil's incentive in completing the task (I), i.e. the extent to which the pupil will feel a sense of pride in completing the task. Weiner explains that, in a model due to Atkinson, these factors are regarded as multiplicative:

$$M = nAch \times P \times I$$

In this model the incentive value (I) is taken to equal $1 - P$ (i.e. the greater the chance of success (P), the smaller the incentive value of the task (I)). It follows that:

$$M = nAch \times P \times (1 - P)$$

This in turn implies that the task which is likely to generate the greatest degree of motivation to achieve is one on which the pupil judges his or her chance of successful completion to be 50 per cent. This prediction from the model might be helpful in guiding us when we are trying to match tasks to individuals. However, if we work to its recommendations we will naturally expect the pupil to fail sometimes, and must surely plan in advance what our response will be to such failure, for otherwise the pupil may quickly re-assess his or her probability of success on similar tasks and will consequently be less motivated towards them in future. One aspect of the mastery learning model which I will discuss in Chapter 4 deals specifically with this point.

A final comment about tactics related to motivation can be based on attribution theory which is a theory about the explanations which people present to themselves for their success or failure on a task. A general finding is that success and failure are attributed to *ability* ('I succeeded because I'm able'; 'I failed because I'm stupid'), *effort* ('I failed because I didn't work hard enough'); *task difficulty* ('I succeeded because the test was easy'); or *luck* ('It wasn't fair, I revised the wrong stuff').

The kind of attributions that a person makes depends on such things as: the success of other people on the task (if everyone does badly then one is more likely to attribute failure to task difficulty than to ability); one's past pattern of success on similar tasks (if one usually fails then ability attributions are likely, whereas if one usually succeeds but fails on a given task, luck, task difficulty, or effort attributions seem probable); the relationship between the work put in and the result (effort attributions are particularly likely if one succeeds after spending a lot of time on the task or if one fails after spending very little time); the randomness of success and failure within the group taking the task (an individual is likely to make luck attributions for his or her own success on a particular task if there is no link between the usual levels of performance of people in the class and their performance on that task).

It is commonly pointed out that these attributions can be classified in two ways: there is an internal/external dimension, and a stable/unstable dimension. For example, ability is an internal/stable characteristic; luck is an external/unstable characteristic.

Pupils will recognise that they (normally) have no control over task difficulty for the task is designed by the teacher; they clearly have no control over luck; they are likely to feel that they have no control over their ability. It follows that if they tend to attribute their failure on a task to one of these factors, there is no logical reason why they should expect to be able to improve their performance on the given task. Furthermore, if their attributions are in terms of ability or luck, they will feel that there is nothing that they can do to bring about greater success on *any* task. The logical conclusion would then be that there is no point in making any further effort in school. Raviv and colleagues (1980) has shown that disadvantaged children are particularly likely to attribute failure to internal causes over which they have no control (e.g. ability) and that they therefore display what he called 'a behaviour of helplessness'. The one attribution that does not lead pupils into this trap is that of effort. If pupils believe that their success is dependent on the effort which they put in, then there is a basis for future engagement in the tasks that are presented to them in school.

Attributions can therefore affect future motivation for school work. It follows that if, as teachers, we can affect the attributions that our pupils make, then we should certainly seek to do so. From the discussion above it would seem to be very much in our interests to promote effort attributions. Being both internal and unstable, effort is the one attribution that leaves the pupil with a sense of control over what might happen next, and personal responsibility for the quality of their own school work.

From the discussion above of how attribution arises, one can speculate that pupils will only attribute success or failure to X if they see a relationship between success or failure and the characteristic X. They would not of course analyse it explicitly in these terms, but in effect covariance will be a crucial influence. Thus if pupils known to be able, always succeed, while those known to be less able, always fail, pupils in general may attribute their own success or failure to ability; if pupils always succeed when they work hard, but always fail when they do not, then they may attribute success to effort, and so on.

If we want to encourage effort-based attributions, this presents us with a problem for it is hard to know how much effort pupils are making. It is therefore difficult to ensure that pupils do well when they have put in a lot of work. Certainly, norm referenced marking of pupils' work (particularly homework done when the teacher is not present to observe the pupils working) is unlikely to reflect the effort made by individuals. A pupil may have struggled hard, but may produce wrong answers and therefore attain low marks; yet, on another occasion, the pupil may dash off a piece of work, get it right and be rewarded with high marks. Such a pupil would see no link between effort and outcome, and would therefore have no evidence to encourage her to make effort-based attributions. Also, the fact that norm referencing implies that a pupil's mark will reflect the level of performance attained by the *other* pupils in the group will do nothing to ensure that an individual's marks reflect their own personal effort.

As long as criteria are well judged in relation to pupils' abilities, it is possible that criterion referenced marking may give rise to marks which reflect effort. At least the influence of the results of the other pupils on an individual's marks is removed. However, careful matching of criteria is not easy and some pupils may work very hard without mastering the next level in a criterion referenced scheme, and will therefore get no reward for their effort.

One suggestion, therefore, is that instead of norm-referenced or criterion-referenced marking, we should mark work against the pupils' *own* previous standards. The reasoning is that pupils will do well or badly in terms of their own normal standards according to the extra effort or the reduced effort that they will have given to the task we are marking. If we award marks that reflect their variation against their own norms, these marks will generally be high when their effort has been high, and low when their effort has been low. There will be a link between mark and effort and therefore pupils will be encouraged to make effort attributions.

Another possibility is that we might ask pupils to write about the way they tackled a task as part of their work on that task. For example we might have asked them what interested them about the task, what surprised them, what they did when they got stuck, what puzzled them about it. Their answers to these questions might well help us to estimate the effort put in to a task as well as encouraging them to take an overview of their problem solving which might well have cognitive payoffs in its own right. These insights into effort could then be rewarded with effort grades.

Assessment of pupils' work has, of course, to serve other ends and effort-related grades will not be the only assessments that we will need to make. If effort grades are given alongside other forms of assessment, it will be important to ensure that they are valued by the school and that this is apparent to the pupils. Perhaps reward systems (such as house points, or commendations from senior staff) should be based only on effort grades.

A further interesting insight is offered by Ames and Ames (1981) who have noted that competitive classroom environments (setting *socially* determined norms rather than criterion referenced ones) can emphasise ability and luck attributions and accentuate both the positive effects of success (which is helpful to the teacher) and the negative effects of failure (which is not). They feel that individualised goal and reward structures, and by implication a more individualised approach to classroom organisation, are more likely to emphasise effort attributions than will the competitive classroom.

A final idea is that of the teacher taking responsibility for pupils' failure. In this model, when a child does badly against the criteria which we have set for a lesson or a test, we say (or imply) that this has happened because we have made an error (we taught the work badly, or gave them a badly constructed worksheet, or whatever). In this way we protect them from ability-based attributions of failure. If we then give them time and support to succeed on what they had previously failed, we may hope to encourage effort attributions. Much of the mastery learning methodology which I will discuss in Chapter 4 could be seen in these terms and the effort-based attributions encouraged could be one reason for its success.

Attribution theory is still the subject of debate at the theoretical level and at the empirical level – in the sense that there is not always clear experimental evidence for some of the very plausible points which are made. It is, however, interesting in its own right, it does raise questions about routine practice in schools, and does offer useful (if tentative) insights for teachers.

Tactics related to insights from information processing models (instrumental enrichment)

It is not possible here to give a detailed account of all the separate strategies that might be used to address individual differences in the specific aspects of cognitive functioning that were described in the section in Chapter 2 on information processing models. It is, however, instructive to look at one integrated programme of work for children with a range of problems of these kinds. Such a programme is that of Instrumental Enrichment (IE) (Feuerstein, 1980). Full adoption of the IE programme requires formal training. Some LEAs in England and Wales have arranged for staff to be trained, but this need for training does limit the scope for application of the programme as a whole. However, helpful materials have been produced by some LEAs and by individuals (e.g. Adey et al., 1989a) which are based on the principles of IE but do not require teachers to complete a formal training before use. It is therefore valuable for teachers to know something of IE, whether or not they work with individuals fully trained in the programme.

A basic assumption of IE is that some pupils have difficulties in learning and problem solving because they have not had what Feuerstein calls 'mediated learning experiences'. In their family situation or very early schooling, children have not recognised their ability to learn from what is around them because no one has acted as mediator, structuring, organising, limiting their experiences in order that learning from them becomes a possibility. IE seeks to allow the teacher to alleviate the ill effects of the lack of such experiences.

Feuerstein describes three stages in mental functioning: input, elaboration (the solution seeking stage) and output. He argues that a pupil can experience difficulties in any or all of these stages. He also recognises various modalities for mental functions – that is various kinds of information which are processed (e.g. verbal, numerical, figural-pictorial) – and argues that a pupil may have difficulty with say the input stage when working in the numerical modality.

The goals of IE are to help pupils improve their cognitive function across the range of stages and modalities. For example IE seeks

- to correct cognitive deficits such as impulsiveness, and lack of systematic observation (input phase), lack of 'if–then reasoning' and of hypothesis-testing strategies (elaboration phase) and lack of understanding of terms such as strategy, symbol, equivalent, similar, etc. (output phase and input phase)
- to increase pupils' intrinsic motivation by giving a habit of successful working
- to increase pupils' ability to engage in reflective thinking, and in particular to monitor their own thought processes so as to be more effective in using them
- to improve pupils' attitudes to themselves as problem-solvers

It is immediately apparent that IE makes very good sense in terms of the descriptions of pupils with learning difficulties that are provided by information processing research (see Chapter 2). It is also clear that if IE can be successful in modifying these characteristics, it should result in a raising of pupils' general problem-solving capacity and that should in turn be reflected in higher IQ scores.

The lesson style within the IE programme is well worth considering at some length as it offers helpful guidance to anyone wishing to tackle aims that are similar to those of IE. The full IE programme involves a series of 5×50 minute lessons per week for two years. A minimum time commitment for an IE programme is 3×50 minute lessons per week for this two-year period. A lesson typically involves 10 minutes or so of discussion between the teacher and class to introduce the problems, to explore what the pupils need to know in order to solve it, and to formulate one or more strategies. Then the pupils work on the pencil-and-paper exercise (instruments) largely independent of the teacher. Able pupils might help the less able at this stage, but the teacher intervenes only to guide someone out of an unproductive strategy. The 'instruments' are content-free so as to remove any expectation of failure associated with work on similar content in the past, and to focus attention on the thinking process rather than the content. It is not uncommon for pupils to be working on more than one instrument at a time. This can encourage generalisation of the skills that are being learnt. There is then discussion within the class as a whole of the various strategies that were used by pupils to tackle the instrument, what was good and bad about these strategies, which were the effective strategies, etc. In this discussion pupils are encouraged to say how they overcame any problems associated with their strategy. The lesson also contains a review of the language used so that pupils are alerted to what might be called 'the language of problem solving'. (One of Feuerstein's hypotheses is that by simplifying our language with pupils who have learning difficulties we can deprive them of ways of viewing problems which itself further handicaps them as problem solvers.) Then there is consideration of the application of the ideas discussed in connection with the instrument to school work and to life generally. Feuerstein calls this the 'bridging stage'. Sometimes pupils are asked to consider 'solutions' to the problem which contain errors and can therefore discuss the ways in which errors are made without the emotional load of considering their own mistakes.

It is difficult to give a flavour of the individual instruments without taking up a great deal of space by including actual examples. However, some idea of what is involved can be conveyed by outlining one or two of the instruments. For example an 'Orientation in Space' instrument is designed to develop pupils' awareness of orientation with reference to a person. It requires them to imagine themselves in a particular position in a drawing and to be able to decide what is to their right, their left, ahead of them and behind them. In Piaget's terms, it addresses the ability to decentralise: to see things from another person's perspective. There is need for 'if–then reasoning'

in the elaboration phase. Pupils are required to complete a table in the output phase. Other instruments on this topic point out differences between left–right directions and compass directions.

There are other instruments on temporal relations which encourage pupils to develop an understanding of such things as the sequential nature of time, and the relative nature of time words such as 'late'. This helps to develop the idea that for someone in 1750, 1850 was in the future even though for us it is in the past.

Pupils do work on comparing and analysing pictures which helps to establish the idea that objects can be the same in some respects but different in others. This is a necessary step in building up an understanding of classification. In science we often use classification in order to understand some principle (e.g. we teach classification of material into solid liquid and gases partly so that we can relate the properties of materials to the particle theory). IE emphasises the skills required to do the initial classification and points out the importance of classifying (e.g. to arrange things so that you can find them), and of understanding other peoples' classifications so that you can use their catalogues, dictionaries, etc.

Other topics include work on giving and receiving clear instructions, on family relationships, on logical reasoning, on syllogisms, on identifying problems which have too little data for their solution to be possible, on sets, on numerical progressions; on analogies, and on divergent thinking.

There have been several formal evaluations of the IE programme. In his own book Feuerstein (1980) describes a substantial study involving 218 students of whom 114 were given IE while 104 were given a general programme of subject related enrichment. In a battery of 28 tests, most showed some gain for the IE group compared with the general enrichment group, and in 12 cases these differences were statistically significant. Feuerstein's discussion of these results is quite positive. He claims (p. 367), for example, that 'the evidence is consistent enough . . . to suggest that IE merits adoption in programs that aim at modifying the cognitive structure of low functioning adolescents'.

In an independent study, Arbitman-Smith et al. (1984) reported that 'after one year of IE students commonly show gains of 5–10 IQ points'. Though they stated that gains on achievement tests were found in some but not all subject areas, they did note 'more marked changes in classroom learning and in enthusiasm for learning'. This same finding of modest cognitive gains, but inconclusive subject-related gain was noted by Shayer and Beasley (1987) after a careful experimental study of 12–14-year olds in a special school for pupils with moderate learning difficulties. They also recorded that IE had substantially affected pupils' metacognitive functioning and had improved their ability to tackle novel tasks.

A further evaluation of IE was carried out in five LEAs in England by the Schools Council (Weller and Craft, 1983). This reported pupils' and teachers' views of IE and gave a generally positive impression. For example when teachers were asked to comment on the responses of their pupils to IE, roughly 80 per cent of the points raised were positive ones, and just over 20 per cent of the comments referred to apparent progress on the part of the pupils. Pupils' own views were also positive. When asked to give their reasons for disliking IE, nearly 50 per cent of the comments were 'I like it all'.

There does therefore seem to be a reasonable basis for continuing to take a serious interest in IE. In the context of the individual teacher's response to pupils' learning difficulties, perhaps the sensible thing would be to adopt one of Shayer and Beasley's suggestions and incorporate the basic principles of the programme into the teaching of mainstream subjects. In this respect, one significant thing may well be to make use of the different elements of an IE lesson, including:

- the initial discussion
- the debriefing of pupils' approaches to the task and the evaluation of different approaches
- the explicit attention to language
- the emphasis on bridging from the lesson to other lessons and to general life

Another way forward may be to copy the concern which IE shows for cognitive processes in themselves (e.g. for the processes involved in classification, or observation). The insights which the IE programme can offer in such areas may help, not only with the learning of science process (Attainment Target 1 in the National Curriculum in Science for England and Wales), but also with learning in those content areas which build on these processes. As part of this, we may be wise to try the IE idea of using content free material to establish success in work on a cognitive process, before employing that process in a science context where some pupils may have learnt to expect failure. It may therefore help to do some work on, for example, precise observation in the context of day-to-day life, before requiring pupils to demonstrate such abilities in the context of observation of chemical reaction or of microscope work.

Tactics related to differences in Piagetian stage of cognitive development

Recently, Adey et al. (1989a) have undertaken work which has the goal of accelerating pupils' progress through the Piagetian stages of cognitive development and therefore towards the stage of formal thought. Evaluations of their programme do seem to be encouraging (Adey et al., 1989b). Adey showed that when project staff taught an experimental group the cognitive acceleration programme which he and his colleagues had devised, they had greater gains in Piagetian level than a control group. Also, over a subsequent period of a year in which no further intervention was made, the experimental group developed at the same rate as the control group. Their gains over the whole period of the study were still found to be greater than those of the controls. Similar results seem to be emerging with respect to experimental and control groups taught by 'ordinary teachers'. The tactics which they adopted were inspired by those of Instrumental Enrichment which were discussed in the previous section. It may therefore be that these ideas also offer a means of attending to differences mapped in terms of Piaget's model of pupil development, by accelerating pupils who are at lower stages than would be expected for their age and ability.

Certainly to my mind, such an approach to Piagetian differences is preferable to one in which we strive merely to match work to pupils' different stages of development. That may avoid frustration on the part of pupils who cannot cope with work that might otherwise be above them, but if genuine and sustained acceleration can be achieved, this alternative tactic of matching seems to be too modest in its aims.

Tactics related to differences in cognitive style

A considerable range of cognitive style dimensions have been identified in the literature. Several of these were mentioned in Chapter 2. Some of their implications for the tactics we might adopt in our teaching can be illustrated by considering just one of them: the holist–serialist dimension. In the study of holist and serialist learners (Pask, 1975), it was clearly demonstrated that students at both extremes of this particular style continuum learnt most effectively when taught in ways that matched their own preferred style of learning. It was not that students using one of the styles were markedly better than the others, just that they were different, and responded to different kinds of teaching.

Teaching particularly supportive of serialist learners would emphasise the logical connections within separate strands of a topic. It would stress the interrelationship of the ideas within one strand and the evidence which is supportive of those ideas. It would stress the details of how things are done. For example, it would explain the details of experiments done to test an idea. Only as a fairly late part of the teaching scheme would the teacher begin to put all the strands together to give an overview of the topic as a whole. A holist treatment might begin with an overview and deal with elements of each strand in ways that stress the links between them. Details of any procedures involved (e.g. exactly how a particular quantity might be measured) would be left until a late stage.

Thus a serialist treatment of basic electronics might deal with the properties of the light-dependent resistor and might use Ohm's Law to generate an understanding of how it can be used in a voltage divider circuit to produce voltage changes as a result of changes in light intensity. Such a circuit might be built and tested. A similar treatment might then follow for a thermistor. Work on current amplification in a transistor might then be done, and an Ohm's Law argument might be used, together with this idea of current amplification, to show how a transistor can be made to operate as a NOT gate and a NOR gate. Circuit elements might then be combined to produce systems to do particular jobs (e.g. to warn of temperature drops at night). A holist approach might look at several applications such as night-time temperature alarms and identify the fact that there are transducers and active circuit elements in all of them. Analogies might be drawn between the light-dependent resistor and the thermistor in that both can be used in circuits to produce voltage changes when there are environmental changes. The properties of NOT and NOR gates might be investigated and analogies drawn between them (e.g. truth tables can be established to enable us to predict what output condition will be produced from various input conditions). Frequent reference might be made to a range of applications using similar transducers and logic circuits. Only at a late stage might the analysis of components in terms of Ohm's Law be attempted.

While it is easy to see how one might teach in both these ways during a piece of educational research on tactics related to learning style, it is asking an enormous amount of a teacher to prepare materials for a class on a day-to-day basis so that both styles of learning can go on. Apart from the investment of time and the complex class management circumstances that would arise, we have to remember that not all pupils can be readily classified as holists or serialists. Instead, many lie somewhere near the middle of the dimension and have no very clear preferred style. Even when pupils do have a clear preference, we may not know enough about their learning styles to be confident in placing them in the correct category.

Some of these difficulties could be overcome by offering the pupils choice over which approach they wish to follow, but there are other problems that would not be avoided in this way.

These arise from the fact that both styles have shortcomings. The holist may fail to value the detailed analysis of the components and may leap to unsubstantiated generalisations, whereas the serialist may fail to recognise the analogies between different components, and may not recognise the interrelationships between the parts of the topic, nor its more general significance (Entwistle, 1981). It might not be enough simply to circumvent any adverse effects arising from the mismatches in teaching and learning styles by allowing pupils to work in their preferred style. It might be necessary to include some element of remediation in the approach. In this, we would not be trying to change a pupil's preferred style, but to add facility in the other styles so that appropriate choices could be made as to which style to adopt in any given circumstance.

One approach related to this view might be to vary our teaching from one topic to another so that pupils would meet all styles. They would, at least for some of the time, be able to follow their preferences, but would also be encouraged to develop more facility in their less preferred style, and would therefore be helped to overcome some of the shortcomings of their preferred style. In an interesting discussion of the widespread effects of the field-dependence–field-independence dimension, Witkin (1977) makes a similar case for a variety of approaches. He states that: 'Beyond encouraging teachers to adapt their teaching to students as they find them, we may hope even more that teachers may find ways of helping students diversify their learning strategies.'

Psychological differences – summary

In the previous sections we have been considering both remedial and circumvention tactics in relation to psychological differences amongst pupils. For example, we have explored remedial tactics through which pupils can be helped to change so as to be more effective in monitoring their own problem solving. We have also considered circumvention tactics, for example those through which we can help pupils with different preferred learning styles to learn more effectively even though we may not be trying to change their learning style as such. Remedial tactics do dominate the section, partly because psychological characteristics which interfere with school learning are often alterable, and are undesirable in that they also affect other aspects of the pupils' functioning. Nevertheless, the importance of circumvention should not be underestimated.

However, perhaps the main point to be made in summarising this section is that, taken as a whole, it encourages us to recognise that we must attend to individual differences in *all* aspects of our teaching:

- it can influence our attitudes to pupils and to their successes and failures (pp. 69, 73; see also pp. 48 et seq)
- it draws attention to our general approach to pupils and their work (p. 70)
- through the notion that motivation is likely to be highest when pupils perceive themselves to have a 50 per cent chance of success at a task, it provides guidelines on what might count as a good match between task and ability (p. 71)
- it provides guidance on specific teaching tactics (e.g. pp. 70, 74, 75, 76)
- it encourages us to adopt a range of assessment tactics in order to encourage effort-based attributions (p. 73)

The section therefore helps to reinforce the notion that attention to individual differences must permeate our whole approach to teaching. It is not simply the production of a few extra worksheets with simpler language for less able pupils!

TACTICS RELATED TO ABLE PUPILS

So far in this chapter, little seems to have been said about meeting the needs of pupils whose educational and psychological characteristics encourage us to classify them as 'more able'. It is important to recognise that this is not, in fact, the case. Many of the tactics which we have been considering apply just as much to these able pupils as to those who have difficulties in learning. For example, the alternative frameworks used by able pupils may be much more sophisticated than the work which we intend to cover with the class. If we do not pay attention to the able pupils' frameworks we may generate a sense of frustration, or even undermine their confidence in their own more advanced ideas by seeming to contradict them in discussing simplified models. Readability tests can help just as much (and just as little!) in the selection of material for unsupported use by able readers. DARTs activities can help to make difficult text accessible to able pupils even though they would not normally be expected to read it. Explicit discussion amongst a group of able pupils of their personal strategies in solving the mathematical aspects of some science problem can extend and develop the range of approaches to mathematics that are then accessible to any one of the pupils. The cognitive modifiability tactics exemplified earlier by reference to Instrumental Enrichment can be used to help able pupils develop advanced approaches to thinking at an earlier age and can give them even greater awareness of their personal methods of problem solving which might help them to extend their range of approaches. Able pupils, like others have preferred learning styles and although an aspect of high ability may be one's better capability of learning in ways that are not one's preferred approach, it may still be helpful to able pupils if the teacher does take some account of their preferred learning style.

These points indicate how the tactics discussed in the rest of this chapter can help able pupils to build upon their strengths. In addition, able pupils may well have some aspects of their functioning which are less well developed than others. The tactics discussed above will then serve a remedial function for those pupils, just as they would for someone with more generalised learning difficulties. A particularly significant example here is that tactics related to motivation may be very relevant to the underachieving able child.

The main work of describing tactics relevant to able pupils has therefore already been covered. Nevertheless, it may be helpful to add one or two points which can be drawn from the literature which is specifically concerned with able pupils. Perhaps the overriding point is that provision should be planned on some explicit basis and should not be simply a series of unrelated tasks chosen because, at some general level, they appear to be intriguing. Tannenbaum (1983) states this very sharply. He argues: 'Differentiated education (for the gifted) is not just a grab-bag of goodies . . . (but has to be) . . . selected carefully to implement a comprehensive plan that has its own built-in rationale . . .'

One helpful means of choosing or designing enrichment materials for able pupils which do conform to some overall structure, is Bloom's (1956) taxonomy of educational objectives – particularly that part of the taxonomy relating to the cognitive domain. Bloom lists objectives in order of increasing cognitive demand. The main headings of his list are:

- knowledge
- comprehension
- application
- analysis
- synthesis
- evaluation

It is logical to assume that material for able pupils should emphasise objectives at the more demanding end of this taxonomy and should therefore stress tasks of analysis, synthesis and evaluation. Though even this is a useful rough guide, study of the full taxonomy is rewarding for there are ordered lists of objectives under each main heading through which one can gain insights into, for example, the kinds of comprehension objectives which are particularly relevant for able pupils.

Renzulli (1977) mentions another basis for the design of tasks for the able pupil. In his Enrichment Triad Model he recommends that pupils should have access to a wide range of interest-provoking activities (Type 1 Enrichment) and to means of developing more advanced study and thinking skills (Type 2 Enrichment). Thus many pupils may find it valuable to learn how to use a school library catalogue, whereas able pupils may be offered Type 2 Enrichment focused on use of professional abstract journals and index journals. The use of Instrumental Enrichment with able pupils would fit in as Type 2 Enrichment. In the past, particularly in USA, activities designed to enrich the divergent production (creativity) aspects of Guilford's Structure of Intellect Model have been common features of Type 2 Enrichment. Renzulli's Type 3 Enrichment is in many ways the most interesting part of his model. This is enrichment based on real-world problem solving, preferably undertaken for a real purpose outside rather than simply as a classroom task for the teacher. Renzulli argues that the complexity of the variables involved in a real problem, the need to identify and solve the methodological problems inherent in real investigation, and the demands implied in producing answers for an informed and potentially critical audience outside the school, are all factors which make such tasks eminently suited to more able pupils. Type 3 Enrichment might involve a survey of children on school meals for the school meals supervisor, or an exploration of some aspect of local history for a presentation to the local history society, or a contribution to work on some problem encountered in a local science-based industry undertaken for the company concerned. Type 3 Enrichment emphasises the pupil as a creator of ideas not merely as a consumer.

A comprehensive and scholarly summary of ideas of this kind related to able pupils can be found in Tannenbaum (1983).

Much valuable enrichment for able pupils can be done within normal lessons, as part of a system of differentiated teaching for all pupils. However, there is value in very able pupils meeting to work together on some issues from time to time. A single class may not provide these opportunities for there may be only one or two very able pupils within it. Renzulli's Type 3 Enrichment clearly lends itself to such out-of-class work. Teachers committed to differentiating normal teaching might, therefore, wish to consider ways in which opportunities for such 'able groups' (consisting of pupils from one school, or from a number of schools) could be established. Teacher involvement in such groups can provide considerable insights into the very high levels of work of which some pupils are capable. As well as the tasks themselves being valuable to the pupils, these insights for the teacher can be useful in informing the design of enrichment material that that teacher might use in future in their own differentiated classroom.

CHAPTER 4

Responding to pupil differences: some possible classroom strategies

The HMI survey of newly qualified teachers (HMI, 1982) states that 26 per cent of secondary school probationers felt themselves to be less than adequately prepared to teach the more able, 38 per cent felt under-prepared to teach the less able, and 26 per cent felt in need of more help to teach mixed-ability classes. There is therefore clear evidence of the need to support newly qualified teachers in this aspect of their teaching. There is also evidence that this need is not limited to the newly qualified. Although now quite old, HMI reports on mixed ability teaching (HMI, 1978) and on secondary education in general (HMI, 1979) make it clear that, in the 1970s, the practice of a substantial proportion of experienced teachers in differentiating work for the whole range of their pupils required development. Undoubtedly there have been advances in this area supported by such recent projects as TVEI, but there is evidence that the problem is still one which is high on teachers' own agendas. In a small-scale survey conducted in 1989/90, a colleague and I found that some 40 per cent of experienced science teachers in 21 schools reported significant difficulties in providing for the whole range of pupils in their classes (Postlethwaite and Reynolds, 1990). This result was confirmed in a similar study of another sample of teachers in the subsequent year.

Although the earlier chapters of this book provide a way of conceptualising such issues and offer direct suggestions for means through which teachers might respond, it is dangerous to assume that ideas of these kinds are all that is needed. Other research provides a strong hint that something more fundamental may be called for. For example, Calderhead (1984) reports that teachers often ask questions of able pupils at the start of the lesson to help to get the lesson going on a positive note, and to indicate the level of response that will be expected of pupils generally. Less able pupils may be asked questions if the teacher want to re-assess the pace at which the lesson should go. Able pupils would be asked again if the pace was getting too slow. Calderhead also refers to Lundgren's idea that teachers judge the pace of their teaching by assessment of individual pupils' attainments by using a 'steering group' consisting of the 10th to 25th percentile of pupils in a class. There would therefore seem to be evidence of teachers using their knowledge of pupils differences to help them control the work of the class as a whole, rather than to address the individual pupils' needs directly. This may be perfectly understandable given the constraints faced by a single teacher attempting to keep a class of thirty or more pupils together, so that the whole group can be involved in the same activities in each lesson. It follows, however, that changes in the teacher's strategy for overall classroom management may be necessary if a more appropriate approach to individual differences is to be achieved, and if the teacher is to be able to make use of the tactics so far discussed in this book.

One possible strategy is a fairly conservative

one: namely to build a great deal of variety into our whole-class teaching. We might use the earlier ideas to identify a range of approaches to teaching, and a range of levels of treatment, that might suit the needs of the different pupils in our class. However, we might not attempt to match work to pupils in ways that address their differences at an individual level. Instead, we might continue to work in a class-focused way but would deliberately choose to teach any given topic by using as many of these ideas as possible over a sequence of lessons, possibly repeating the key aspects of the topic in different styles and at different levels as part of this strategy. In this way we would hope to enable all pupils to learn about the topic because each could tune in to the aspect of our teaching that suited them. A simple example of such an approach is to ensure that instructions for an experiment are written out, and described verbally, and modelled by the teacher going through a 'dry run' of the work with the apparatus. This would provide suitable input for pupils who prefer an aural presentation to a visual one; it would support pupils who have reading difficulties; it would help the pupils who lacked a specific piece of knowledge (e.g. the name of a particular piece of equipment). It would do all these things without the teacher having to identify the pupils with these different characteristics and target the relevant tactics on each. A more complex example of this kind of approach would be to devise both a holist and a serialist approach to a topic and ensure that both were taught to the whole class, perhaps over a series of lessons.

This general strategy does offer some possibilities, and may certainly be one way in which teachers can gain personal experience of some of the tactics mentioned earlier without committing themselves to major change in their classroom organisation. However, it is unlikely that this strategy would enable us to go far enough to support the whole range of pupils in our classes (particularly those with special needs), there is real risk that it would add to the problem of lack of challenge for able pupils, and it can be seen to be inconsistent with some of the tactics which could not therefore be incorporated into it.

Flexible learning

A much more radical approach is that of flexible learning (Employment Department, undated) which has been the subject of considerable recent development under the auspices of TVEI. In this document (p. 4), two fundamental aims of flexible learning are expressed:

1 'to meet pupils' learning needs as individuals through flexible management and use of a range of learning activities, environments and resources'
2 'to give pupils increasing responsibility for their own learning and development.'

As conceived by the authors of the Employment Department paper, these aims of flexible learning are met through a situation in which the teacher is not the sole (or even the most significant) source of information for the pupils. Instead pupils learn from a wide range of resources including printed materials, computer-based material, audio and video programmes, and people other than the teacher inside and outside the school. The teacher's role has several elements. It is to ensure that appropriate resources are available in the classroom, in the school library or resource centre, and also, where appropriate, outside school. It is to ensure that pupils develop the skills to access these, including the skills to make use of the support which can be provided by, for example, library staff. It is to engage in negotiation with pupils (in small groups and, at times, as individuals) to help them to set targets, and where necessary to clarify these targets so that each pupil knows exactly what they are aiming for in the next block of work. As part of the basis for this negotiation, it is the teacher's role to have a clear framework of aims and objectives for the course, including notions of what is and what is not negotiable with pupils within this range of objectives. In this way, decisions made with individual pupils can remain coherent, and sensitive to external demands such as those of the National Curriculum, while still giving those pupils some influence over their work. The teacher's role is also to monitor pupils' work, and, in partnership with them, to record their progress towards agreed targets. Through this monitoring process, recognition should also be given to any incidental learning that the pupil can demonstrate has taken place. Another element of the teacher's role is to provide feedback and to encourage pupils to develop self-appraisal skills. A further important aspect of what the teacher does is to encourage pupils to take an increasing share of responsibility for all these aspects of their own learning.

In relation to the differentiation of work within this kind of flexible learning framework, a significant element of the teacher's role is to ensure that there is sufficient range in the resources that are available, and in the activities based on them, to enable all pupils to learn effectively (albeit, perhaps, at different rates). The teacher will also help pupils to focus on the tasks and resources which are most appropriate for them during the negotiation phase of flexible learning. In doing so, the teacher will take account of their own view of the pupil's strengths and weaknesses, but will also respond to the pupil's personal interests and perceived needs. It is, however, an open question as to whether, in the teacher's own plan for the course, the basic aims and objectives for all pupils are the same, or whether differentiation of aims and/or objectives is made.

Careful preparation of a range of resources and tasks, direction of pupils to appropriate tasks for them, and detailed feedback on the work that is completed, may well be the most significant aspects of the teacher's contribution to the individualisation of pupils' learning. However, another way in which teachers can respond to individual differences within a flexible learning framework is to organise personal support or extension for a pupil once they are embarked upon an agreed task. Such support will include help from the teacher to remedy or circumvent a problem where a learning difficulty arises, and will include discussion to enrich the most able. Compared to systems of whole-class teaching, flexible learning may make such support a more realistic proposition. However, the time demands of the other aspects of the teacher's role within flexible learning should not be underestimated and the opportunities for

extended work with individuals or small groups may still be relatively limited. Teachers may also support pupils in their work on agreed tasks by organising contacts between the pupil and other specialists such as special needs staff. This will be necessary when the help required by a pupils goes beyond the teacher's expertise, or requires a greater investment of time than the teacher can properly give in the light of their responsibilities to other pupils in the group. The teacher may also seek to help a pupil to make (and use) contacts with specialists in industry, or in higher or further education. Such contacts may have expertise in a particular field which will be valuable when, for example, it is appropriate for an able pupil to go well beyond the normal objectives for the course.

All of the ideas outlined in the first chapters can inform the teacher's thinking and action in relation to these kinds of differentiation. They indicate the dimensions which should be involved in the planning of differentiation, and the kinds of tactics which should be built in to the differentiated materials. They should inform the way in which the teacher conducts the negotiation of tasks with the pupil. It may be helpful to look, in a little more detail, at how this might be done.

In terms of the differentiation of resources, some helpful insights are provided by Powell (1991) and Waterhouse (1983). Both stress that resources are likely to be published material of some kind, as the preparation of high-quality resources from scratch is so time consuming that few teachers would have the opportunity to create their own. They suggest that although there will probably be a range of resources on any topic in a flexible learning classroom, it is unlikely that all aspects of differentiation can be catered for by the range that is available. This is partly because of the expense of providing books, computer programs and audio-visual material appropriate to the whole range of pupil differences, and partly because it is by no means certain that the necessary range of resources exist. However, in the model that they describe (which, in both cases, is based on that of the Resources for Learning Development Unit in Avon) the work that pupils do with these resources is directed by 'task cards'. These are relatively short documents which are usually produced by the teacher. Task cards do such things as

- set specific objectives
- guide the pupil towards the resources which are suitable for use
- specify (with varying degrees of open-endedness) what the pupil is to do with the resources
- suggest the kinds of output the pupil should produce as a result of the work

There can be a range of task cards for each aspect of a topic so that pupils with different strengths and weaknesses can be given tasks which are well matched to their personal characteristics. There may therefore be a variety of routes through a topic.

In a very simple version of this idea, all pupils may begin with a common task card. The next task may be differentiated into three levels: there may be enrichment for those who have already covered the key points on the topic, further mainstream work for those who are coping with the main ideas, and support for those who have demonstrated a lack of understanding. All three versions of this second-stage task may refer pupils to the same basic resources but they will be using those resources in ways that suit their own needs.

The nature of the tasks required, and the amount of support provided, by the task cards are therefore important and practicable means by which the teacher can deploy a wide range of tactics to meet individual needs, even when the range of resources to which the cards refer is relatively limited.

Powell (1991) gives some very clear and very helpful advice on the design and layout of task cards, but neither he, nor Waterhouse, gives an extended discussion of the theoretical constructs which might offer a teacher guidance on the details of matching tasks to pupils. I would argue that this is where many of the ideas from the earlier chapters of this book can profitably be used. For example:

- a range of task cards could employ differently structured DARTs activities to enable pupils with varied levels of understanding of a concept such as that of growth, to learn from the same biology text book or video tape
- in teaching the notion of, say, chemical reaction, different task cards could help pupils with different alternative frameworks conduct experiments which would appropriately challenge their way of thinking
- different task cards on a topic could take a holist or serialist approach to that topic
- a set of cards might deal differently with the mathematical aspects of a topic: one of these might provide extensive help with the mathematical aspects of 'floating and sinking', by directing pupils to a spreadsheet to conduct an investigation of role of density so that they can appreciate the principles without getting held up by the computations involved. Another card on the same topic might take pupils through an algebraic proof of Archimedes Principle. Both of these task cards might refer to the same resource material on floating – one perhaps using it as an end point of the investigation work, the other using it as a starter for the more theoretical treatment
- enrichment task cards could build an emphasis on the higher levels of Bloom's taxonomy (analysis, synthesis and evaluation) into the tasks required of able pupils

With its recognition that learning takes place in contexts other than the classroom, flexible learning also lends itself very readily to Renzulli's idea of Type 3 enrichment.

There is, then, plenty of scope for incorporation of many of the ideas of the previous chapters into the resources, and more especially into the task cards, that are an important element of a flexible learning approach. I would not wish to pretend that the preparation of differentiated task cards will be a trivial task for the teacher, but it is certainly more realistic than producing differentiated resource material.

Other ideas from the previous chapters can be used in the negotiation phase of a flexible learning approach. The basic framework of Chapter 2 can help the teacher to think clearly about what should go on in any tutorial sessions with individual pupils: to recognise the dimensions of diagnosis that may be required, and to act in logical fashion on the information that such diagnostic investigation might reveal. The small group or individual tutorials then provide an excellent setting for the teacher to deploy the tactics from Chapter 3. For example, in this setting it is certainly possible for the teacher to explore pupils' alternative frameworks and to recommend work to challenge the pupils' ideas. Subsequent tutorial meetings will give the teacher the opportunity to use the tactics recommended by Nussbaum and Novick (1981), by Hashweh (1986) and by others to consolidate the changes in thinking made by the pupils. Where tutorials are conducted with small groups, there are excellent opportunities to encourage pupils to compare and discuss their strategies for solving problems and therefore to make explicit the metacognitive agenda on which systems such as Instrumental Enrichment (Feuerstein et al., 1980) place so much emphasis. The notion of negotiated tasks and of negotiated assessment provide the context in which it may prove possible to deploy the tactics described in Chapter 3 which relate to pupils' self-esteem and motivation. Finally, the whole flexible learning approach, and particularly perhaps the periods of negotiation, emphasise a general classroom environment in which the teacher is very much 'on the learners' side'. This is just the sort of supportive environment for which, from different theoretical perspectives, there were repeated calls in the work reported in the previous chapters.

In a very similar way, the whole range of tactics from the earlier chapter could inform any individual support which the teacher is able to offer pupils during their work on agreed tasks. One of the things which prompted my own interest in this field was the recognition, as a fairly new teacher, that I actually had few specialist tools that I could use during those rare opportunities at lunchtime or after school when it was possible to do some extended work with individuals who were having difficulties. I found that I was effectively limited to the same kinds of explanations that I used in class. While the chance for increased dialogue may well have been supportive to the pupils, I was very dissatisfied with the scope of the teaching tactics which I could deploy. Chapter 3 does, I hope, go some way to suggest tactics that may be appropriate. Flexible learning does make more opportunities available, within ordinary lesson time, to deploy them.

Although flexible learning does not, in principle, preclude periods of whole-class teaching, some versions of the approach do imply that pupils will make progress at very different rates over long periods of time so that, after, say, a term, individuals in a class can be expected to be at very different points in a prescribed course (Employment Department, undated). This, of course, makes it difficult for the teacher to find topics for whole-class teaching that are relevant to all the pupils at the same time. Waterhouse (1983) offers a way around this problem in that he implies that work should be divided into topics. Typically, the teacher introduces each of these topics by means of whole-class teaching, then pupils use resource-based study to work on the main learning objectives of the topic as individuals or in small groups. To conclude the topic, the teacher may work with the whole class to summarise the work, encourage an interchange of ideas and perhaps conduct a summative assessment. In this model, the negotiation of tasks and the individual support and enrichment that I have discussed above are part of the resource-based phase of each topic. The opportunities which this sequence brings for whole-class teaching not only adds variety to the pupils' experience, it also allows the teacher to exploit the strengths of the whole-class approach (e.g. its power to stimulate interest in a new topic through direct communication of the teacher's personal enthusiasm for the topic and sense of its importance for the pupils, or more simply by providing pupils with an impressive demonstration). What is more, it does this without the drawback for the teacher of having to teach in this demanding way four or more times a day, five days a week. In this version of flexible learning, the teacher does not have to contend with an increasingly complex management problem as time progresses, and the pupils become more and more widely spread over the course.

Mastery Learning

In the version that had just been described, flexible learning has something in common with Bloom's model of Mastery Learning (Bloom, 1976) which offers a theoretically coherent strategy into which we can fit much of what has been said so far in this book. Both flexible learning and Mastery Learning are strategies for the differentiation of work for all pupils in a class. They both offer a framework for support for pupils with special educational needs but they do not apply simply to this group of pupils. They therefore exemplify one of the basic principles of this book: namely that provision for special needs should not be added on to an otherwise unchanged approach to teaching.

The core ideas of Bloom's model are that all but the most severely handicapped children, the brain damaged or those with severe personality problems, have the basic mental equipment to cope with school learning. The success or otherwise of pupils in a particular learning task will depend, not on their psychological resources but on

- the pupils' previous learning in related areas
- their attitudes and feelings towards the task currently being required of them
- the nature of the learning task itself and quality of the instruction which they are offered

It is therefore a model which is predominantly based upon educational differences (though, as we shall see, insights related to differences of other kinds can be drawn into the model in a helpful way). Bloom's assertion is that if pupils have the necessary prior knowledge and positive attitudes to learning the subject, and if the learning tasks and the teaching are well designed, almost all pupils can be successful in their learning. He claims that under the appropriate conditions, and for the expenditure of some 20 per cent of additional time, approximately 80 per cent of pupils can master

work which, under conventional teaching only 20 per cent would be able to master. This startling claim implies that pupils with a wide range of IQ can be helped to meet common course objectives. Mastery Learning is therefore a very good example of the point which I made earlier: namely that in non-conventional methods of teaching, the strong link which we have come to expect between IQ and attainment can be broken. In that it claims to break the grip of IQ on pupils' attainments, Mastery Learning is a radical approach to teaching and learning. However, in terms of its classroom organisation it is perhaps less radical than those versions of flexible learning in which pupils are allowed to progress at their own rate over a substantial period of time.

Mastery Learning encompasses the idea that the course we offer to pupils should be divided into units each of which represents up to approximately 10 hours of work. For each of these units, the criteria for mastery should be clear: that is, the pupils (as well as the teacher) should know what is expected of them at each stage. Each unit is planned to take account of what the pupils, as a group, already know and can do, so that pupils are not presented with totally unrealistic tasks. This may imply that some preliminary work will be necessary before the unit proper is begun, or that the teaching approach will be chosen so that some missing skill or piece of prior knowledge is no longer a handicap to the pupils. Although, in describing his model, Bloom did not make explicit reference to pupils' alternative frameworks, it would seem sensible to include concern over this aspect of pupils' prior knowledge in the requirement that work should be planned take account of pupils' starting points.

Once a unit of work has been defined, the first treatment of the ideas within it is through the normal range of teaching methods. This would include whole-class teaching, practical work, demonstrations, work on text books and problems, role play, discussion, use of audio-visual resources or any other method that forms part of the teacher's normal repertoire of work with whole classes. At the end of this first treatment of the ideas, there is a diagnostic assessment to see if each pupil has attained the unit objectives and, if not, to indicate what help is needed. This assessment is not used as part of the teacher's accumulating record of pupils' attainments: it is simply a diagnostic instrument.

The most significant thing about this assessment is that although it is at the end of the first treatment of the ideas that comprise the unit, it is not at the end of the unit as a whole. Instead, on the basis of the assessment findings, pupils who have not attained the unit objectives are given the help they require, and any additional time they need, to achieve such mastery; pupils who have already attained the objectives are given enrichment work focused on new objectives that relate to the topic but do not merely accelerate them forward to work which the whole group will have to consider at a later date. The work that follows the diagnostic assessment is designed on an individualised basis and may very well deploy the whole range of flexible learning approaches that have been outlined above. It may therefore involve a resource-based approach with tutorials in order to negotiate with pupils the support or enrichment programmes on which they are to work. It is therefore at this stage of the unit that Mastery Learning makes opportunities for the teacher to bring into play the whole range of tactics which we have been considering.

Ideally, time would be spent on this individualised phase until all pupils had attained the key unit objectives which were defined at the start. In practice, the teacher may have to make a decision to move the class on to a final summative assessment of the unit and then on to the next unit before this has been fully achieved.

It is inevitable that early units in a Mastery Learning sequence will take longer to teach than would be the case under conventional instruction. However, this need not be a major problem if we take the view that what really matters is the quality of the *learning* that pupils achieve. There is little point in being able to teach more quickly under conventional instruction if little is actually learnt. Mastery Learning provides a system which helps to ensure that effective learning is achieved through the expenditure of the additional time required. It is also important to note that, in a sequence of units that are to some extent inter-related, the more secure learning of early units will help to reduce any additional time requirements for later units.

Mastery Learning emphasises pupils' prior understanding of the topic. It takes account of pupils' attitudes to the learning of the subject. It is based on a unit structure that is decided by the teacher in terms of the subject content. Much of the work is teacher-led. The diagnostic assessment, and the consequent enrichment and support are all related to the subject content of the unit. All of these factors are open to influence from the teacher. Thus, within a Mastery Learning model, learning is held to be very much within the control of the teacher. The approach is therefore in direct contrast to the idea that pupils' learning depends on characteristics such as IQ which are often assumed (perhaps wrongly) to be fixed and therefore to lie outside the teacher's influence. Mastery Learning can, then, be viewed as an exciting and challenging description of learning because it suggests that teachers can affect the learning of pupils to a much greater extent than is sometimes thought. However, this same feature can be seen as very threatening by teachers, because it does essentially put the responsibility for pupils' success, and for their failure, firmly on our shoulders.

Bloom claims that Mastery Learning will raise the attainment of pupils and that there will be less variation from one pupil to another in the scores achieved on summative tests focused on the main course objectives. (Pupils engaged in enrichment tasks during the individualised phase of the model will, however, learn additional things so the model implies no 'levelling down' of the most able.) In his book (Bloom, 1976) he presents evidence from a number of studies which supports these claims. In some studies the amount of time available to teachers to learn about Mastery Learning before teaching within it was relatively small; in others teachers were working with large classes of up to 70 pupils. These were not, therefore, favourable results achieved in absolutely ideal conditions.

Research on Mastery Learning has been quite extensive since Bloom's own reports. Guskey and Gates (1986) provide a useful and fairly up-to-date summary. They carried out a meta-analysis of 27 such studies, choosing those which they could demonstrate had been well designed. They reported generally positive effects from the Mastery Learning approach: pupils in Mastery Learning classes did better than those in conventional classes; they spent more time on-task; they had better attitudes and more positive views of themselves as learners of the subject; they retained their learning for longer; their teachers had more positive attitudes, and higher expectations of their pupils in Mastery Learning classes. The effects of Mastery Learning seemed to be somewhat smaller in secondary classrooms than in primary. The authors speculated that this may have been because the longer exposure of secondary school pupils to conventional teaching strategies had resulted in more gaps in understanding or in poorer attitudes towards learning on the part of the pupils. Alternatively, it may have been a consequence of the fragmentary nature of the secondary curriculum. They also reported effects to be smaller in science and mathematics than in other subjects (but this was possibly because the pupils involved in these studies tended to be older and therefore the subject result was coloured by the age result already mentioned).

In a more direct survey of pupil opinion on Mastery Learning, Geeslin (1984) showed that 78 per cent of a sample of over 1000 pupils liked working in this way. This held across all age groups in the sample and in relation to almost all subjects.

Finally, Fuchs et al. (1986) showed that Mastery Learning was particularly effective when careful attention was paid to the diagnosis and corrective teaching element in the model. This finding reinforces the proposition that careful development of support and enrichment is essential and that attention to the ideas of the first chapters of this book may therefore be valuable. It also suggests that Mastery Learning is a good framework in which to attempt to put such ideas into practice.

I will try further to clarify the nature of Mastery Learning by discussing some aspects of an investigation into its use which some colleagues and I carried out with PGCE students at Reading University as one part of a small scale research project funded by the Employment Department. At the beginning of this chapter, I indicated that local science teachers felt they needed to develop their approach to differentiation in science teaching. In an attempt to address this, a group of two university tutors, two teachers and three PGCE students developed a Mastery Learning module which was then trialled by a larger group of students during their teaching practice. The module consisted of a lesson sequence for pupils in Year 10 and was concerned with the skills of 'planning a fair test'. It was set in the particular context of an investigation into the factors which affect the rate of photosynthesis. We provided a lesson plan for an initial whole-class treatment of the topic. This had five clearly defined objectives. We provided a simple diagnostic worksheet for use at the end of this whole-class phase of the topic. Questions on this worksheet were directly linked to each of the five objectives. We then provided support materials relevant to each objective to help pupils who had not mastered the objective during the whole-class phase. Finally, we designed some enrichment materials which were intended to extend pupils basic mastery of the process of experimental design through consideration of more complex issues related to this topic.

We introduced the student teachers who were to trial the module to the concept of Mastery Learning by means of the flow chart shown in Figure 4.1, and through the associated notes which are included as Appendix 1. We emphasised to students that all pupils are involved in this model. It is not just used for very able pupils or those with learning difficulties.

We then provided details of a lesson plan which would serve as Stage 1 of a module dealing with the problem of designing a fair test of the effect of varying light intensity on the rate of photosynthesis in pond weed. The objectives which we defined for this module were that pupils should demonstrate:

Figure 4.1 Flow chart for a Mastery Learning module on 'Planning a fair Test'.

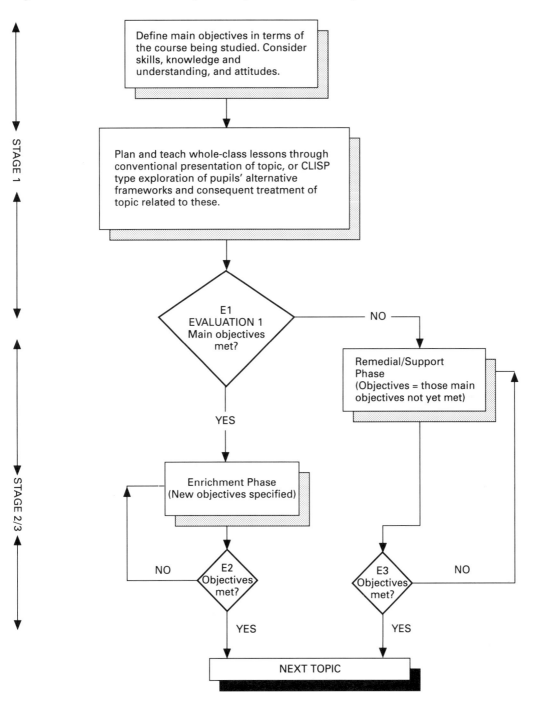

1 Understanding of what is meant by a variable by identifying the relevant variables in the particular case of the photosynthesis experiment.
2 Ability to identify the dependent and independent variables in the photosynthesis experiment.
3 Understanding of the importance of controlling variables and how this can be done in the photosynthesis experiment.
4 Ability to choose appropriate ways of measuring the variables of interest in the photosynthesis experiment.
5 Ability to select appropriate apparatus and use it to achieve (3) and (4).

Part of the lesson plan was a simple worksheet which would enable the teacher to judge how far each of the pupils had achieved these objectives.

We also provided material for the Support Phase of Stage 2 of the flow chart. There was support material relating to each of the five original objectives. Students were encouraged to use the insights provided by pupils' responses to the worksheet to direct them to the appropriate support material.

Finally, we provided three pieces of enrichment for the Enrichment Phase of Stage 2. Two pieces of material were concerned with the *design* of fair tests; the third required pupils to criticise the design of experimental work reported in the literature. The first made less complex demands than the other two and was designed to accommodate those pupils who were borderline in their mastery of the original objectives. The objectives of the Enrichment Phase of Stage 2 included such things as being able to suggest *possibly* relevant variables in a particular system, even where that system is complex and only limited information is available about it; and being able to recognise or suggest different *kinds* of ways of controlling variables in a particular system.

In Appendix 2, I have included some examples from the support and enrichment materials which we provided. The first is part of the support material designed for pupils who had difficulty identifying relevant variables in the photosynthesis experiment and who therefore did not reach the first of the Stage 1 objectives. The second is a support material focused on understanding the notion of control and applying it to the photosynthesis experiment (the third Stage 1 objective). The final example is part of a piece of enrichment material, deliberately chosen to offer a substantial challenge to able pupils. It focuses attention on the issues of experiment design by asking pupils to analyse accounts of early researches on the topic. It has a further aim of helping pupils to develop a better understanding of the history of scientific ideas and of the processes by which these ideas develop.

In the next section, I shall outline some of the ways in which ideas from Chapter 3 informed the design of these materials.

The Support Phase material which we designed included work intended to help pupils to understand what is meant by the term 'variable' and how they can decide whether a variable is likely to be relevant to any experiment which they are designing. This work was based on familiar everyday situations and drew heavily on ideas from Instrumental Enrichment (IE). The actual example of material provided in Appendix 2a follows directly on from this work on variables and attempts to bridge the pupils' growing general understanding of the notion of variables, into the particular context of the photosynthesis experiment. Because pupils may not start with all the necessary background information to do this, the example provides a short piece of text which presents the key ideas. Pupils are invited to learn from this text by using the DARTs text analysis activity of underlining. Pupils are encouraged to do this cooperatively if possible. Pupils are then asked to use the information they have identified in the text to complete a table. (This is a DARTs text reconstruction activity. As mentioned in Chapter 3, text analysis is generally a good preparation for text reconstruction.) At the end of the example, pupils are asked to make explicit to themselves the processes which they have been through, discussing these with their teacher. This was included in response to the IE notion that pupils need to discuss and evaluate their problem-solving strategies in order to develop those strategies to the full. Simply to practise them is not enough.

The example of work in Appendix 2a is followed, in the full set of materials, by a separate exercise which helps pupils to understand the notions of dependent and independent variable. The example provided in Appendix 2b is the step which then come next: namely that of using knowledge about variables to help in the design of fair tests. In several IE instruments, pupils are asked to analyse examples of some concept, before they are asked to create examples of the same kind for themselves. This sequence is employed in Appendix 2b where pupils first analyse simple examples of fair and unfair tests before being asked to design their own fair tests using very similar sequences of ideas.

The example starts with *analysis* of simple 'test' designs. These move from very familiar situations towards more laboratory-based work and gradually place more emphasis on continuously variable variables where control involves some kind of measurement (not just assurance that, for example, both batteries were new). Pupils are encouraged to use the language of dependent and independent variables to help them in their analysis. They then move on to the *design* of fair tests starting with a familiar context and with the support of concrete equipment to help them explore their ideas. They are then encouraged to use the same kind of approach in the design of the photosynthesis experiment. Again there is an opportunity for a review of their thinking with their peers and their teacher.

Appendix 2c provides an extract from one of the pieces of enrichment material that we designed. Of the three pieces in the full set of materials, the first was a fairly simple extension of the ideas presented in Stage 1. This was provided in recognition of the fact that some pupils who meet the Stage 1 objectives will only just have done so, and will need to consolidate rather than significantly extend their understanding. The second piece was a more demanding, requiring students to apply what they had learnt about photosynthesis, and about the design of fair tests, to a consideration of an experiment on the efficiency of food production. This was intended to move towards Renzulli's Type 3 enrichment, though we did specify the task fairly tightly and did not set it up with a real audience in mind for the pupils' work. The material of which Appendix 2c is an extract, was the third, and most demanding, of the alternative enrichment materials. It focuses on objectives related to the higher orders of Bloom's taxonomy. It is intended to help pupils to see how ideas about photosynthesis developed over time, and to reflect upon the experiment design decisions that were taken by the earlier researchers. It draws attention to the role (sometimes the limiting role) of existing knowledge in the design decisions that scientists take. It could be used by the teacher to build up to a discussion of the nature and status of current scientific understanding.

These examples show how some of the ideas from Chapter 3 can influence the design of teaching materials and approaches. The opportunity clearly exists for many more of the ideas to be built in to Mastery Learning materials, and into the ways teachers negotiate tasks with pupils, work with them to overcome specific problems, and review the learning which is achieved.

As I explained earlier, the full set of these materials were trialled by a group of PGCE students during their teaching practice. Their comments on the materials are interesting. It is important, however, to note that they had to fit in trial of the material to their teaching practice circumstances and were not able to control the conditions of their own experiment in ways that one would normally expect in full scale educational research. (For example, some students had to trial the material with pupils who were either much older, or much younger than the Year 10 target group.)

Eight of the 12 students who returned full evaluation forms reported that the strategy (as summarised by the flow chart) was easy to understand. Ten students stated that the strategy was sufficiently flexible that they could adapt it, and the materials which we had designed, to cover similar work on fair tests in a context other than that of photosynthesis. One pointed out, however, that this took 'a considerable amount of work'.

Eleven of the 12 felt that the materials which we had produced were closely related to the strategy and that, in consequence, their function and interrelationship could be readily understood.

Two students reported that all of their pupils had mastered all of the Stage 1 objectives after the initial whole-class treatment of the ideas. Two reported that none of their pupils had achieved this. For most of the students, between a third and half their pupils had completed all the objectives after Stage 1.

Seven students commented on the different parts of the material. Six found the enrichment material 'sufficiently challenging', whereas one reported that they were too difficult. Five found the support materials sufficiently challenging. One student reported that 'they seemed trivial in some cases but produced the required results'. However, two students felt that they were too easy.

Seven students also attempted an estimate of the extent of pupils' enjoyment of different aspects of the Mastery Learning approach. Five reported that pupils enjoyed the Stage 1 activity, four that pupils enjoyed the enrichment and three that pupils enjoyed the remedial tasks (with one additional student saying that she was not sure about enjoyment, but she did feel they had not understood the purpose).

Finally, students commented on ways in which their trail of the materials and/or the underlying Mastery Learning strategy had informed their own thinking about differentiation. Some of these comments were quite helpful for anyone intending to explore mastery learning, and such comments are listed in Table 4.1.

I would not wish to suggest that the student teachers' experiences outlined above represent a hard-line evaluation of Mastery Learning, but they do perhaps indicate something of its potential, and its problems, as a strategy into which a wide range of remedial, circumvention and enrichment tactics can be fitted. The comments therefore repay some further consideration.

The general comments relate quite well to the key points about Mastery Learning that have already been mentioned. The reference to the importance of matching the initial activity to pupils' attainments is significant. In discussion, students reported that where that match was not good, many pupils failed to meet any of the objectives during Stage 1. They were then engaged in so much support work in Stage 2 that they began to tire of the materials. Where Stage 1 left most pupils with only one or two objectives to address through the support materials, interest could be sustained and the sequence worked well. This is an important reminder that the presence of the support phase is no excuse for insensitive planning of the original content and treatment of the topics.

The reference to the need to group pupils during Stage 2 is another interesting point, which is stongly supported by Waterhouse (1983) in his discussion of the practicalities of class management for flexible learning.

The need for tact, and the problem of pupils feeling inferior if they were directed to support materials were points that were strongly felt by some student teachers. Some of the support materials that we had designed went back to very simple situations based on everyday experience. 'The Race' in Appendix 2 is perhaps one example. Clearly, one way to avoid the risk that pupils will be insulted by such work is if the simpler objectives are addressed in earlier years so that only on rare occasions would an older pupil need to go back to material that starts from such a simple starting point. Perhaps another key to pupils' feeling good about work of this kind, where it *is* necessary, is their recognition that they really do learn by using it. Thus, the first exposure to Mastery Learning may well be more problematic in terms of pupils' reactions to the materials than later sessions when pupils can refer back to the earlier successful experience of being helped to tackle something which they at first found difficult. It, is incidentally encouraging that the pattern of failure and success that may accompany Mastery Learning was reported, in work summarised in Chapter 3, to be helpful in encouraging high levels of motivation amongst pupils.

The final point which I would like to pick up from the record of students' views is their com-

Table 4.1 Student teachers' comments on insights gained from the use of the Mastery Learning strategy and materials

---

General comments

Before I used the materials, I only understood in principle. The materials gave me a practical understanding.

You have to plan how to decide who does what activity and whether this is to be teacher or pupil directed.

Thought and time must go into differentiation.

The (Stage 1) activity must be accessible to most pupils and form a larger part of the lesson.

You must ensure that all pupils feel that they have understood a new topic and have been kept fully occupied.

Differentiation requires a lot of planning. Pupils can be bored by too much of the same.

Evaluating pupils' understanding is difficult.

Flexibility is required. Groups need individual attention. Pupils doing less demanding tasks can be resentful of those doing harder things.

The techniques can be applied to any lesson.

You need tact to ensure that pupils using support material do not feel inferior.

You cannot have all the pupils working individually. You need to group them in order to deal with the questions.

It is difficult to predict how pupils will respond to this approach.

Try not to label the pupils.

About enrichment materials

They shouldn't be too difficult.

(The examples showed) the extent that is possible given time.

It is more difficult than providing support material: it must extend their skill and knowledge, not be too difficult, be relevant, be interesting.

Must be interesting, challenging and relevant. It is more worthwhile if it is directly related to the topic. It is helpful to include a practical element.

Materials are good for motivated pupils. Others see them as extra work.

They need to be tailored to the individual and not be too much of the same.

About support materials

They should not be too easy.

(The examples showed) the extent that is possible given time.

They must be stimulating, and must not make the pupil feel inferior.

They are useful as revision and back-up.

They need to be presented seriously, with carefully chosen examples.

You need to find out who needs what support. Avoid giving too much of the same material.

Pupils do not like going back to the Stage 1 worksheet (i.e. the diagnostic assessment sheet).

---

ment that pupils did not like going back to Stage 1 materials after the support phase. As the reader can see from Appendix 2, we used this tactic at the end of each block of support material, once an objective from Stage 1 had been met. The intention was to help pupils to recognise that they had now mastered something which they previously had found difficult. The fact that student teachers found this a problematic notion suggests that pupils were misinterpreting the intention here. In Mastery Learning it is valuable to let pupils into the 'secret' of the model so that they are quite clear about the different stages and what they can expect to get out of them. If 'return to the diagnostic assessment worksheet' is perceived to be 'do the test again because you got it wrong' all is lost. If, however, it is perceived to be 'go back and fill in the answers you didn't get because you have now got that problem beaten', then perhaps the demotivating aspect will disappear.

The brief descriptions of flexible learning and Mastery Learning hopefully give insights into how the mainstream science teacher can move towards fuller differentiation of work within the classroom. It is important to point out that they are both styles of classroom organisation which greatly empower special needs staff and adults other than teachers who may be available to offer support, in the mainstream classroom, to pupils with special educational needs. Such staff are greatly limited in what they can do for pupils if the predominant teaching style is one of whole-class teaching. However in the resource-based phase of the models of classroom organisation that we have been considering, it is much easier for support staff to find situations in which they can work with special needs pupils without interrupting the flow of the lesson for others. Also, since the general context is one in which all pupils are working on a range of tasks, it is easier for support staff to make use of their specialist expertise, and their specialist resources within the mainstream classroom, without marking out special needs pupils as being significantly different from the rest of their classmates. If such support is to be of greatest effect, it is clearly important that science staff and support staff communicate with one another over the objectives of the topic, the content to be covered and the likely difficulties of the special needs pupils. This is often said in relation to all in-class support scenarios, but in practice it is extremely difficult to find the time to follow the advice. In this respect both flexible learning and Mastery Learning have further advantages over conventional teaching. First, more of the planning has to be committed to paper (e.g. in the resources and task cards that are necessary). Staff can therefore share ideas without always having to meet face to face. Secondly, negotiation of tasks is part of the lesson structure. If support staff join in the negotiation which takes place between pupil and the mainstream teacher, the necessary staff to staff interchange can take place *as part of the lesson* rather than as an extra for which (usually) no timetabled time is made available. Certainly in the early stages of any staff partnership some opportunities for other discussion may still be necessary, but these occasional meetings are perhaps manageable even within a busy schedule. What flexible learning and Mastery Learning do offer is time within the normal lessons with a class to do the day-to-day discussion about the support of individuals within that class. It is this regular staff contact that is otherwise so difficult to organise when all staff are so heavily committed.

Summary

This chapter, and its two associated Appendices, should have suggested some ways in which we could organise our general approach to teaching so that it becomes possible to make use of the ideas which emerged from the earlier chapters of this book. It should also provide some indications of the kinds of ways some of those ideas could be applied to the topics of the science curriculum.

There is no doubt that the development of any of these approaches is a massive undertaking for any individual teacher. It could, however, become a more realistic undertaking if a department, with appropriate support from special needs colleagues, were to plan to develop the necessary resources incrementally over a long period of time. Mastery Learning (perhaps more so than those systems of flexible learning in which the topics of pupils' work tend to become more and more different as time goes on) does lend itself to piecemeal development topic by topic. Initial work is likely to be quite protracted and difficult, especially if a team of colleagues have to begin to come to terms with the idea of mastery learning as they produce their first sets of material. However, some support material will have application to a wide range of topics and therefore has more than a single use. Development tends, therefore, to become less traumatic once some initial experience has been gained.

For teachers considering whether to take the first steps down the Mastery Learning road, perhaps one more finding from the student teachers who trialled our material would be helpful. Several of the student teachers stated they only really began to appreciate that the Mastery Learning material had value when they actually tried it with pupils. The most harsh criticisms came from students who had only gone so far as to read and discuss the ideas.

CHAPTER 5

Putting the ideas to use

One thing is clear about the previous chapters of this book: they are largely concerned with principles, and with empirical results, which are claimed to have some sort of generalisable application to the issue of the differentiation in science teaching. They offer theory-based and research-based suggestions for ways in which we might *think* about differentiation, and ways in which we might *act* to differentiate our teaching. Another thing should be clear: namely that the chapters have been written with the intention of helping to improve our practice, as teachers, student teachers and teacher educators, in relation to this aspect of our work. Given these points, it might be helpful to finish with a brief consideration of the links between theory and practice so that readers will then be better placed to make use of the book in relation to their own teaching.

An interesting starting point for this is provided by Wilson (1975). He draws attention to the tentative nature of much of the theory which is held to be of value to teachers and suggests that one should therefore use theory cautiously in a context as important as education. (This point is important, but it can be overstated as the tentative nature of theory in the physical sciences does not stop us from applying that theory to the design of bridges and aircraft and the radiological treatment of disease.) More significant, perhaps, is the fact that in educational contexts, several theories from a given discipline, or theories from a range of disciplines, might be relevant to any given situation. These different relevant theories may very well have different, or even contradictory, implications. Therefore, there is indeed a significant risk in assuming that any *one* theory can be used directly to prescribe what teachers should do. In response, one might argue that theory should be ignored. However, Wilson warns of the 'wholly disastrous' nature of this assumption. He suggests instead that an open-minded, critical reading of 'theory' might help teachers to clarify issues, question 'commonsense' suggestions about practice (which may be common but not, actually, very sensible) and gain insights into alternative practices which might (just might) be helpful in their own classrooms. Readers should find that this book can be used in precisely these ways: not as a recipe for practice but as one source of ideas that might help in the creation of a given teacher's (or a department's, or a school's) approach to the issue of differentiation.

This view of the treatment of theory in educational decision making is taken further by McIntyre (1988) who argues that student teachers learning to teach (and, I would add, experienced teachers striving to develop their teaching) should test ideas which are intended to inform practice against a wide range of criteria. He states that these should include criteria closely related to the concerns and situation of the particular school in which the teacher is working (e.g. the resources available in terms of equipment, teaching spaces, support staff and the like; the attitudes and expectations of colleagues, of parents, of governors and of pupils, the recent history of that school and department). He argues that they should also include criteria such as 'the intellectual clarity and coherence of the theory underlying the proposed approach, the educational values implicit in it and its general effectiveness in achieving its intended purposes as reflected in the research evidence' (McIntyre, 1988, p. 109).

One might clearly treat this book as a collection of 'ideas intended to inform practice' and subject it to just this kind of analysis in order to establish how it might best be used to inform the development of practice in a given school. I will make no claims for the 'intellectual clarity' of the text, but I feel it is reasonable to argue that there is a sense of coherence in much of what has been presented in the previous chapters. Also, the text includes reference to empirical evidence to establish the 'general effectiveness' of the ideas. In analysing the text against such criteria, different teachers may be more convinced by some elements of it than by others. However, even where teachers agree on how the different parts of the text measure up to examination in terms of these theoretical criteria, the importance of the more context-specific criteria listed by McIntyre suggests that they may each come to regard different ideas as worthy of trial in their own particular teaching situations. In follows that different teachers, and certainly teachers in different schools, may use the same material to create different approaches to differentiation. Each of these approaches may well be right for that particular teacher to try in their given setting. For example, a teacher who has the support of special needs staff in the mainstream classroom may feel that the team of adults in the classroom will be able to give an adequate amount of personal attention to small groups of pupils working on different aspects of a topic. Such a teacher may find the arguments for a heavily resource-based approach to differentiation less convincing than a teacher who has to think of ways of attending to individual differences without the support of another adult in the classroom. Similarly, if timetables are such that each teacher teaches in one room for most of the time, a resource-based approach where pupils work at their own pace over long periods of time and begin to spread out over many different topics may be regarded as

manageable whereas, if the teacher has to move resources from room to room, such an approach may be viewed as totally impracticable. The general validity of the ideas in the present text does not prevent each context-driven decision from being the correct one for the teacher involved. It follows that the context-specific validity of one particular idea for one particular teacher does not prevent the other ideas from being valid for other teachers, or indeed for the same teacher should their contextual circumstances change.

Far from being a prescription for action, the present text may therefore be seen as a starting point for the *creation*, by teachers, of a range of new approaches. Each of these should then be tried out to determine their validity in the relevant local context.

In addition to the criteria provided as examples by McIntyre, one might argue that it is important to test any set of ideas or practices against the implications of all the relevant theories. From this perspective, the book can be seen as an annotated catalogue of some of the theories and research relevant to differentiation.

For example, one important reason for drawing attention to Guilford's multidimensional theory of intellect in Chapter 2, is not that the Structure of Intellect model provides a recipe for what we should do in schools, but that it encourages us to be critical of simplistic notions of pupil grouping. If it is possible for pupils to have strengths and weaknesses across a range of aspects of intellect, and if different aspects of intellect may be related to performance in different subject areas, how can we justify streaming pupils in a school so that each pupil is in the top, or middle, or bottom stream for every subject? We may argue instead for setting, or may claim that no system of selection can be sensitive to the whole range of strengths and weaknesses that our pupils may display and find that a compelling reason for mixed ability grouping.

Used as a source of theoretical ideas, which relate to differentiation, and which could be used to encourage critical analysis of a school's, or a teacher's, policies and practices, the book will still not dictate what that particular school or teacher should do. This is partly because of the points raised earlier.

First there will often be a wide range of 'relevant theories' against which ideas or practices should be tested. In relation to the example of setting and streaming, a school may feel that although setting is desirable on the basis of Guilford's model, there are good sociological, or social psychological reasons for streaming or mixed ability grouping on the grounds that these alternatives allow pupils to settle down in a consistent class group, whereas setting places pupils in different groups for every lesson and disrupts peer relationships.

Then there will be local practical constraints. A school may agree that setting is theoretically the most defensible approach, but argue that streaming is nevertheless the best solution in its context as setting is organisationally too complex given its particular staffing constraints.

Then there will be local institutional history which will also matter. For example, in a school which has just been formed by the amalgamation of two schools with rather different ability ranges in their intakes, setting might tend to perpetuate classes that existed in the old schools, so the school may decide to adopt a mixed-ability grouping system, largely to help establish the identity of the merged institution.

For all these reasons, arguments may be found which may well prove more powerful than those which can be based upon Guilford's model. The present treatment of Guilford's theory does not then guarantee the adoption of any one grouping system. It does, however, add an important dimension to the debate, it makes our decision making more explicit, and it alerts us to some of the possible consequences of the decisions that are finally taken. It may, for example, warn us that if we do adopt streaming for some reason, then we should expect to find some individuals in each streamed group for science who have particular strengths or weaknesses in abilities relevant to science, and are therefore more able, or less able in that subject than their group placement would otherwise lead us to expect. This in turn may make us more aware of the need to differentiate

teaching within each streamed group, and may weaken any inappropriate self-fulfilling prophecies that we may otherwise be inclined to make.

Though Guilford's model and its implications for pupil grouping provide a convenient example which can be discussed relatively briefly, I would suggest that all of the theoretical ideas and empirical findings discussed in the previous chapters can be used in the same way by those who have to take decisions about aspects of differentiation. They all have value in adding to the range of considerations which we can take into account.

The reflective practitioner

These ideas have much in common with those of Schön (1983, 1987), who developed the notion of the role of reflection in the development of professional practice. He argued that professionals reflect-in-action in producing the moment by moment decisions that governed expert performance in rapidly changing circumstances (such as those of the busy classroom). He also argued that professionals reflect-on-action during those moments after the event when we consider what went on and try to plan more appropriate responses to similar situations that might occur in the future. It is a mark of enormous expertise to be able to make use of information such as that provided by the earlier chapters, together with a knowledge of other relevant theories and of local constaints and opportunities, in order to reflect-in-action on issues related to differentiation. Where this is possible only to a limited degree, or where longer term planning decisions are involved, it is valuable to reflect-on-action.

Louden (1991) has offered an interesting framework which we can use to consider what such reflection might mean in relation to this book. First he argues that anyone proposing change in teachers' practice is likely to have more impact if there is an element of continuity between current practice and the developments which are being proposed. This continuity brings not only a sense of familiarity which is likely to make the new ideas seem plausible to the teachers, but, more significantly, it signals a respect for their current practice as being a generally well-judged response to current circumstances. In other words, it indicates that teachers' practice may need development given new insights but is not so inappropriate that revolutionary change is the only solution. I would argue that Mastery Learning, the overall teaching strategy which I feel has much to offer those who wish to improve their approach to individual differences, stands in just this kind of relationship to much current practice in teaching. It is radical in some of its principles (e.g. that almost all pupils are capable of learning things which we might otherwise regard as within the scope of only a few) but there is considerable continuity in its proposed teaching methods (e.g. that much of the instruction is whole-class teaching and that even the more individualised phases are controlled by and paced by the teacher). I feel that many of the other ideas in the book can also be seen as evolutionary, rather than revolutionary.

Secondly, Louden identifies what he calls different *interests* for reflection which are closely related to different goals for the process of reflection. The first is 'technical reflection'. The goal here is to establish how well practice matches some specification of what that practice should be. If teachers were to adopt Instrumental Enrichment in full they would, I suspect, feel it necessary to engage in technical reflection to ensure that their practice measured up to the quite detailed model of how specific instruments within that programme should be used, and how IE lessons generally should be conducted. However, the notion of technical reflection carries with it the notion that there can actually be a detailed specification of practice that must be followed. As the previous discussion shows, I am not inclined to see most of this book in these terms. I therefore feel that technical reflection has relatively little to offer in terms of guidance on how to use it.

Louden's second interest for reflection is 'problematic reflection'. This is reflection focused upon a specific problem in the classroom. I feel that the book has much more to offer here. For example,

a teacher may find that as a term progresses able pupils in a class are beginning to show signs of restlessness and boredom. In reflecting upon possible causes the teacher may begin to question the appropriateness of the work being demanded. The analysis offered in the section on able pupils may well be useful here. For example, it draws attention to Bloom's taxonomy as a basis for the design of genuinely challenging enrichment materials, and recommends that such materials emphasise the higher levels of that taxonomy; it summarises Renzulli's notion of setting able pupils real-world problems to be reported to real-world audiences; it reminds us that able pupils may need to be introduced to higher level study skills if they are to be able to meet the greater demands of work designed to take account of these ideas from Bloom and Renzulli. Other sections may also shed valuable light: for example, the section which deals with motivation may suggest a different kind of analysis altogether. Therefore several areas are offered for exploration during reflection on this particular problem. In different situations the relative value of the different ideas may vary, but the subjects discussed here do offer support for the teacher's thinking and subsequent action. A teacher using the material to support problematic reflection of this kind may simply change some aspect of the way they teach and keep the effect of these changes under general review, or they may see the issue as worthy of more detailed, and more explicit, trial and evaluation, perhaps through the procedures of action research (see, for example, Carr and Kemmis, 1986).

The third of Louden's 'interests for reflection' is labelled 'personal'. In this category Louden places reflection aimed at developing a deeper personal understanding of an issue, and at making more explicit the connections between our professional understanding and experience and the whole range of personal experience which influences our thinking and action. The whole of the present work should be a useful guide to the development of personal understanding. It is harder to give detailed examples of how it might help us to connect our experience and understanding to our personal lives. However, I feel that the broad exploration of the issue of differentiation which it offers may perhaps have potential in helping us to re-examine and perhaps re-interpret earlier experience, and to re-evaluate its implications for future action. A useful methodology for personal reflection may well be that of journal keeping, or of biography writing (Connelly and Clandinin, 1987).

Louden identifies 'critical reflection' as the final 'interest for reflection'. He states that this form of reflection calls into question 'taken-for-granted thoughts, feeling and actions'. Louden explains that critical reflection involves exploration of the circumstances in which professional action is taken. It includes consideration of the contraints which influence that action and encourages the frame of mind in which such constraints are seen as alterable, even though they might often seem natural and perhaps unchangeable. He argues that critical reflection involves consideration of who benefits from current practice, how it might be changed, and what personal or political action might be necessary to bring about such change.

Clearly, a stimulus for critical reflection is a recognition that some practice does not measure up to a view of what may be desirable. By summarising a wide range of theories and empirical findings related to differentiation, this work might serve as a source of ideas of 'what *may* be desirable'. It can therefore help in the identification of mismatches between current practice and desired practice, and may thus help to focus critical reflection.

The result of critical reflection may be a recognition that the mismatch which is under consideration is a consequence of the fact that, say, teachers' interests are being given priority over pupils' interests; or that some timetabling decisions inhibit the adoption of the more appropriate classroom practice; or that some feature of resourcing is the cause. Whether these constraints are seen as alterable will depend on the role which the teacher engaged in the reflection is empowered to play, or willing to play (e.g. as individual teacher, as head of department, or as citizen with the political influence that this offers). I would suggest that critical reflection might also, on occasion, result in a scepticism about the validity of the suggestions made for so-called 'desirable practices'. This might lead the teacher to question the theory on which these suggestions are based, and to generate alternative hypotheses on which new theories could be based.

Summary

I have, then, three main motives in drawing attention to these views on the development of thinking and practice in teaching, and on the role of theory in that process. The first is to guard against any implication that the material presented here should be regarded as a recipe for good practice. Fundamentally, it would be to misunderstand the relationship between text books and professional decision making in individual schools and individual classrooms. Since teachers, quite rightly, tend to adopt a critical stance to theory there is little risk that misuse of this kind will be very widespread.

My second motive is to encourage careful thought about the ideas presented here, even though they may not match current practice and may sometimes seem to be difficult to implement given the common practical constraints of schools and of our present educational system in general. Any such mismatch may be a sign of the potential usefulness of the ideas, not a mark of their weakness. The conflict between the ideas and the common constraints within which we work may be a sign that the constraints need to be changed rather than the ideas relegated to oblivion.

My third motive is to affirm my belief that expert teachers *create* optimum teaching and learning conditions in their classrooms. This book does not seek to replace this process of creation by dictating what those conditions should be in order to attend to the whole range of individual differences amongst our pupils. It *is* intended to inform the process of creation.

Notes on the Mastery Learning strategy*

These notes help to explain the overall strategy illustrated by the flow chart (see Figure 4.1 on p. 89). It is not easy to live up to the specification they provide when designing a specific piece of teaching. Our own example falls short in some respects. However, the notes should help you to understand our example more fully and therefore to use it appropriately.

Stage 1

The objectives for this stage will be based on the course materials that you are using and/or on the National Curriculum. They must be defined clearly as they form the basis of decision making later in the sequence. The teaching and learning activities that are involved at this stage could be those of conventional whole-class teaching, and could include group work or practical work done by all the pupils. Where lessons are concerned with knowledge or understanding, they could also be activities designed to elicit and work with pupils' alternative frameworks.

The first evaluation (E1) is a diagnostic evaluation designed to show which pupils need more time or support to achieve the Stage 1 objectives, and which have mastered these and are ready for enrichment work. This evaluation should not

play any part in any cumulative record of pupils' achievements. It is purely a tool for deciding what happens next for each pupil. You should try to ensure joint pupil/teacher ownership to this evaluation. At least ensure that pupils understand its purpose in the overall strategy defined by the flow chart. In general you could make use of any appropriate form of assessment (e.g. written classwork, oral work, pupil self-assessment, tests, homework) though there is no suggestion that you should use all of these in any one evaluation. The evaluation could be an integral part of the activities of Stage 1. You will need time to reflect on the results of the evaluation before Stage 2 in order to assign pupils to appropriate activities in Stage 2. Ideally this would be done through discussion with small groups of pupils, perhaps while the class as a whole is writing up some aspect of Stage 1.

Stage 2

This is a more individualised stage consisting of two phases: the Support Phase and the Enrichment Phase. Pupils work on one or other of these as a result of the first evaluation (E1).

Care needs to be taken to avoid any notion of labelling the pupils who are tackling the support

---

* As they appear, these notes are a slightly modified version of those provided to the student teachers who were to trial the Mastery Learning materials which were developed as part of the Reading research project. The reader should remember that they were originally addressed to a student teacher group who were cooperating in the research.

phase. They are not 'remedial' pupils; they are simply pupils who need some help on the objectives of Stage 1. Pupils may be asked to tackle the support phase for one topic, but the enrichment phase for the next depending on their success in the respective Stage 1 activities.

There are Support Phase activities related to each of the Stage 1 objectives. Different pupils should be encouraged to work on different subsets of the support materials during Stage 2 dependent upon what they have already achieved in Stage 1.

The enrichment phase has new objectives related to a more challenging aspect of the Stage 1 work. The enrichment phase does not seek to hurry successful pupils on through work which all will be expected to do later. That would merely store up difficulties for later in the course.

Stage 3

This is a second round of support or enrichment activities for those who, by the time the E2 or E3 evaluations are done, have not achieved the Stage 2 objectives on which they have been working. Ideally a wider range of alternative materials may be needed for Stage 3 to cater for all degrees of achievement that have been reached by that stage. In practice, it may be difficult to find time to run Stage 3.

Further notes on the Support Phase

Though the objectives for the Support Phase are necessarily the same as in the initial stage, the teaching method and resources used should not simply repeat the original treatment of the topic. There should be a variety of support resources and routes available to the pupils to match the difficulties which they each have. In the context of the National Curriculum, the design of this phase can make use of lower Statements of Attainment related to our original objectives to give clues to what might be needed as support work. It is, though, important to remember that there is at present no guarantee that the sequence of SoAs

is genuinely developmental so care should always be exercised in using them in this way (e.g. there is no guarantee that SoA4 provides a basis for learning SoA5). Plans for the Support Phase should take account of what is being done in other subjects (e.g. maths). Special needs colleagues might be consulted, especially if more straightforward ideas for this phase fail to work.

Teachers can work with individual pupils in this phase, which provides another opportunity for work based on pupils' alternative frameworks – even if that approach was not part of the original treatment of the ideas. The main principle in the Support Phase is to help the pupils to meet the original objectives, so the work done in this phase might not always seek to improve pupils' basic skills (such as reading or number skills) as such. It might instead help pupils to meet the science objectives despite problems with those skills. Ideas such as DARTs, use of calculators and spreadsheets, and ideas to support concept learning all have a part to play in informing the design of Support Phase activities.

It is easy to bore pupils by too much similar activity in the Support Phase. This can be avoided in two ways: first by ensuring that the original Stage 1 material is at a sensible level for most of the pupils in the class, so that pupils do not have to go over too many basic skills during the Support Phase; secondly by encouraging pupils to work on the particular materials in the Support Phase which match their particular problem. Careful interpretation of the E1 evaluation is therefore important.

Each of the support activities we have devised begin with fairly general references to the relevant ideas. We then try to apply these to the particular situation of the photosynthesis experiment. Pupils may need to be reassured that we are not underestimating their ability by starting with such simple things. It is just that this is an effective way of helping them. The same starting points might be useful as support material for work on 'fair tests' in some context other than photosynthesis. However, if you use them in this way, you will have to write your own materials to 'bridge' from the simple starting points to your particular context.

Further notes on the Enrichment Phase

This phase should not just be about more difficult content. It should relate to skills, cognitive objectives and affective objectives in the laboratory context, or in broader social, technological or economic contexts. The E2 evaluation should test achievement of these new objectives.

In the design of these objectives, and in the related materials, it is important to remember that some of the pupils who will be directed to the enrichment phase will not be extremely able pupils, but will merely have met the objectives of the particular piece of work at Stage 1. At least one piece of enrichment material should be fairly closely linked to the standard of work expected at Stage 1.

Other pupils using the enrichment material will be 'more able' pupils in the usual sense. Such pupils should certainly be helped to apply their science in real-world situations where the range of relevant factors complicates the question under consideration. They should be helped to acquire any advanced study skills needed to meet these demands. Some of the enrichment objectives should make higher cognitive or affective demands on the pupils, such as those defined in the higher levels of Bloom's taxonomy. For all pupils engaged in the Enrichment Phase, the work should not merely be 'more of the same' to fill time, nor should it require pupils to start on the next topic, or on the more advanced treatment of the present topic that the whole class will be expected to do in the future.

Examples of materials used in Stage 2 of the Mastery Learning module explored in the University of Reading research

In the flow chart in Chapter 4 (Figure 4.1; see p. 89), Stage 2 of the Mastery Learning model is identified as the more individualised stage in which pupils are encouraged to work on either support material (if they have yet to master some of the key objectives of the module) or on enrichment material (if they have already demonstrated mastery of those objectives).

In this Appendix, I have provided examples of materials that might be used in Stage 2. These are based on some of the resources prepared for the Support Phase and the Enrichment Phase of the Mastery Learning module on 'designing a fair test' which was developed and trialled at Reading University during 1990/91. The work was carried out in the context of an experiment to investigate the effect of light on the rate of photosynthesis. Despite the setting of a small-scale funded research project, the time available to develop these materials was extremely short and these resources are not offered as exemplars of the best that can be achieved, but merely as concrete examples of ways in which some of the tactics discussed in Chapter 3 of this book can be used to inform the design of work within a Mastery Learning structure.

The resources below consist of:

(a) *part* of the material used to help pupils who had not yet mastered the first objective: namely to 'demonstrate an understanding of what is meant by a variable and to identify the relevant variables in the particular case of the photosynthesis experiment';

(b) the material used to help pupils who had not yet mastered the objective 'to demonstrate an understanding of the importance of controlling variables and how this can be done in the photosynthesis experiment';

(c) examples of the enrichment materials used by pupils who had met all the key objectives at the end of Stage 1 of the module.

(a) Support material – Identifying relevant variables

[Preceded in the full set of materials by a worksheet on identifying variables in common situations.]

What affects the rate of photosynthesis in pond weed? Identifying variables which might be relevant

You were able to base your answers to the last worksheet on your everyday understanding of how things work. It is not quite as easy to think about what affects the rate of photosynthesis. You need to know something about the process to be able to do it. You have done work on this before, but, to remind yourself, **read the next section now**:

Photosynthesis in pond weed

Like other green plants, pond weed can make sugar from carbon dioxide and water. When this happens, oxygen is also made. This oxygen comes out of the plant and can be seen as bubbles in the water around the pond weed. To do this job, the pond weed needs energy. It gets this from the light which shines on it. Bright light provides more energy than dim light. Red light is more easily used by the pond weed than most other colours.

This process of making sugar and oxygen is called photosynthesis.

Pond weed uses the carbon dioxide which is dissolved in the water it is in. The amount of dissolved carbon dioxide can be varied by adding sodium hydrogen carbonate (carbon dioxide solution) to the water. Many other plants take carbon dioxide from the air. The water for photosynthesis is water that is already inside the plant. It is not the water in the beaker holding the plant.

Now go through the passage (with a friend if possible) and *do the following*:

- Underline, in blue, two things which are made if photosynthesis happens.
- Underline, in red, two things the sugar is made from. The pond weed needs these if photosynthesis is to work.
- Also in red, underline one other thing the pond weed needs.
- Draw a ring round the words which tell you where the pond weed gets its carbon dioxide from.
- Draw a ring round the words which tell you where the energy comes from.
- Draw a ring round the words which tell you where the pond weed gets the water it needs for photosynthesis from.

Summary

Now you have most of the information you need to decide on some of the variables which are

important in the process of photosynthesis. The next section will help you to sort this information out.

Using your information

- Look back at your work. The things underlined in red are things that the pond weed needs. *Write them down in Table 1*, in the column headed 'Things needed'.
- Now look at the things you have drawn rings round. These tell you where the pond weed will get things from. *Write these in to Table 1 in the second column*.

Table 1

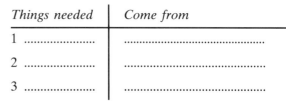

Things needed	Come from
1	....
2	....
3	....

All these things could be changed in some way – all of them are variables. However, it will be difficult for us to change the amount of water inside the plant. *Therefore write down the two most relevant variables* for our experiment:

....

These are two of the things which might have an effect on how fast oxygen gas is produced by pond weed.

Some extra information

Photosynthesis takes place inside a plant. However, it is just a chemical reaction like the ones you see in test tubes. So there is something else which affects how quickly oxygen gas is produced by pond weed. It is something that affects most chemical reactions – the temperature.

- You could change the temperature of the plant. How could you do this?..................................

Also, you would expect the size of the plant to affect how quickly oxygen gas is produced by pond weed.

- You could easily change the size of plant. How could you tell how much you had? ....

This suggests that temperature and size of plant are two more relevant variables.

Summary

You have now identified four variables which you would expect to have some effect on how quickly oxygen gas is produced by pond weed. To get them all together, write them here:

....

....

....

....

- These four variables are the answers to Question 1 on the Student Worksheet that you used in an earlier lesson. Fill them in on that worksheet.
- Now look back through the work you have just finished. With a friend, or in a group, decide *how you found out* that the four variables that you have written down in the list above were the relevant variables. (There are two main steps.) Write down your ideas, then talk to your teacher about what you think.

(b) Support materials – controlling variables

Stage 2 Materials Fair tests

Think about the three tests in the boxes below and *say whether you think they were fair*.

The race

Maria wants to see if Sarah is generally a faster runner than Jean.

She times Sarah over a distance of 100 m downhill. Sarah takes 15 s. She times Jean over a distance of 100 m uphill. Jean takes 20 s.

Maria concludes that Sarah is generally a faster runner than Jean.

Is the race a fair test? ....
If not, why not? ....

Checking the adverts

A TV advert says that a Duracell battery lasts longer than an ordinary battery. Tania wants to see if this claim is true.

She puts a new Duracell battery in a torch and times how long the bulb stays alight.

She then puts an ordinary battery (again a new one) in the same torch and times how long the bulb stays alight.

Is this a fair test of the advert? ....
If not, why not? ....

Bouncers

William wants to see if a marble bounces higher than a tennis ball.

He drops the ball 1 m on to a rubber mat and measures how high it bounces.

He drops the marble 2 m on the a hard floor and measures how high it bounces.

Is this a fair test? ....
If not, why not (give two reasons)?

....

Some information

To design a fair test you first decide which variables might be relevant.

You then decide which of these variables you are going to affect directly (the independent variable), and which you are going to measure when the experiment responds (the dependent variable).

Finally, you have to decide how to keep the other variables the same while you do the whole experiment. This is so that there are no unfair influences of the results.

Keeping the other variables the same is called *controlling* the variables.

Did you think about this when you criticised the three tests?

Check your thinking against the ideas below and fill in the missing word or words wherever there is a line (_____).

The race

In the race, the independent variable was the person. The dependent variable was their speed. But the track could also affect the runners.

Maria should have kept the track _____ (uphill for both runners, or downhill for both runners). She should have controlled the track. She didn't, so it wasn't a fair test.

Checking the adverts

In the battery test, the independent variable was the type of _____. The dependent variable was how long it would last for. But the _____ of the batteries and the job they were doing could affect how long they would last.

Tania did keep these things the same (they were both new batteries, and she tested them in the _____ torch). She did control the age of the batteries and the job the batteries had to do. It was a fair test.

Bouncers

In the bounce test the independent variable was the type of ball. The dependent variable was the _____ of the bounce. But the height of the drop and the kind of floor the balls land on could affect the bounce.

William should have kept these the same. He should have controlled the height and the _____ surface. He didn't, so it _____ a fair test.

Remember:

Controlling a variable means doing something to make sure that this variable stays the same through all the parts of the experiment.

All of these ideas help you to tell whether a test is fair or not.

They also help you to design your own tests.

You are going to do that next.

Designing two fair tests

You want to see which of three saucepans heats up quickest

A set of apparatus is available to help you think about the experiment. You can use this in any way you like to help you with your design.

You do not have to carry out the whole experiment.

The independent variable is the type of pan. The dependent variable is how quickly the pans heat up.

- What will you measure to see how *much* a pan heats up?

  ....

- How can you measure how *quickly* it heats up?

  ....

- What variables might affect how quickly the pans heat up?

  ....

- How will you keep them the same (control them) while you test all three pans?

  ....

You can use the same kinds of ideas that helped you design a fair test of the pans to design a fair test of the effect of light on photosynthesis. Next we take you through the steps.

You want to see how light affects the amount of oxygen gas that is produced by pond weed in one minute

- What will you measure? ....
- How will you do this?

  ....

- What variables, apart from the brightness of the light, might affect how much oxygen gas is produced by pond weed in one minute? (You have already done some work on this and got the answers right. Check back if you have forgotten.)

  ....

- How will you control these variables while you test the different strengths of light?

  ....

  ....

The last two lines above are the answer to Question 4 on the Student Worksheet you will have used in an earlier lesson. Fill in the worksheet.

You have learnt a lot about scientific experiments. Check up on what you have learnt by talking to your group and then writing down what you think the following terms mean.

an independent variable ....
a dependent variable   ....
controlling variables   ....
a fair test   ....

When there is a chance, talk to your teacher about your design for the experiment on photosynthesis. Tell them especially how you made sure it was a fair test.

(c) An extract from Enrichment Material

Taking things further – analysing experiments

Introduction

Plant nutrition has been investigated by scientists for centuries because of the importance of growing plants for food. The essential process in plant nutrition is photosynthesis, yet it was not until the nineteenth century that scientists could give an accurate description of the raw materials and products of photosynthesis.

This worksheet outlines the major advances made in the investigation of photosynthesis during the period 1648–1804.*

It is interesting to see how a scientific explanation developed over time as people devised more sophisticated experiments and took account of knowledge from other aspects of science. We hope you will enjoy the materials from that point of view. However, we are mainly interested in what they can help you to learn about experimental design.

We would like you to try to work out why the early experimenters did what they did, and to be critical of the experimental design that they used. We would like you to think why they came to conclusions that we now think are wrong.

We will ask you some specific questions after each piece of text, to get your thinking started.

Jean Baptiste van Helmont (1577–1644)

One of the earliest investigations into the raw materials and products of photosynthesis was carried out by a Dutch physician, Jean Baptiste van Helmont. He did not know about photosynthesis as such, he was simply investigating the raw materials from which vegetable matter was formed. One of his reports is entitled 'By experiment, that all vegetable matter is totally and materially of water alone'. This was published by Ortus Medicinae, Amsterdam, in 1648.

---

* The material is based on ABAL, 1983, *Energy and Life*, Cambridge University Press.

You can read part of this report in *Energy and Life*. (For the convenience of the present reader the extract is printed opposite.) Do this now.

After your reading, discuss the following points with a friend and make some notes on your ideas

- Why did van Helmont use dried earth to set up his experiment? (There is a hint towards the end of his passage.)
- Why do you think he used rainwater or distilled water – what was he trying to control for?
- Why do you think he was concerned about dust, and what do you think of the things he did about this?
- The fact that van Helmont omitted to measure the weight of the leaves that fell off each autumn did not affect his conclusion. Why not?
- van Helmont left any consideration of light out of his design – why do you think he might have done so?
- What do you think about his conclusion?

(Similar work is then suggested in relation to other historical accounts of experimental investigations)

'By experiment, that all vegetable matter is totally and materially of water alone'

'I took an earthen vessel, in which I put 200 pounds of earth that had been dried in a furnace, which I moistened with rainwater, and I implanted therein the trunk or stem of a willow tree, weighing five pounds. And at length, five years being finished, the tree sprung from then did weigh 169 pounds and about three ounces. When there was need, I always moistened the earthen vessel with rainwater or distilled water, and the vessel was large and implanted in the earth. Lest the dust that flew about should be co-mingled with the earth, I covered the lip or mouth of the vessel with an iron plate covered with tin and easily passable with many holes. I computed not the weight of the leaves that fell off in the four autumns. At length, I again dried the earth of the vessel, and there was found the same 200 pounds, wanting about two ounces. Therefore 164 pounds of wood, bark and root arose out of water only.'

Van Helmont's conclusion could be summarised as a word equation:

$$\text{water} \xrightarrow{\text{vegetation}} \text{vegetable matter}$$

The SMOG Readability Formula

- Select 10 sentences from the beginning of the text you wish to use, 10 from the middle and 10 from the end.
- Count the number of polysyllabic words (i.e. words with three or more syllables) in all 30 sentences. Call this number n.

  (The number of syllables in a word is the number of vowel sounds that make up the word. People sometimes disagree on the number of vowel sounds in some words as this will depend on pronunciation. An adequate approach for the SMOG test is simply to say the word and count the number of vowel sounds in your pronunciation.)
- The Readability Score for the text is $8 + \sqrt{n}$. For the interpretation of readability scores, please refer to p. 63.

Bibliography

Adey, P. et al (1989a) *Thinking Science, the Curriculum Materials of the CASE Project.* London, Macmillan.

Adey, P. et al (1989b) Cognitive acceleration. In P. Adey et al (eds) *Adolescent Development and School Science.* New York, Falmer Press.

Adey, P. and Shayer, M. (1990) Accelerating the development of formal thinking in middle and high school students, *Journal of Research in Science Teaching*, 273: 267–85.

Ames, C. and Ames, R. (1981) Competitive v. individualistic goal structures, *Journal of Educational Psychology*, 73(3): 411–18.

APU (1982) *Science in Schools Age 13: Report 1.* London, HMSO.

APU (1988) *Science at Age 15: A Review of APU Findings 1980–84.* London, HMSO.

APU (1989) *National Assessment: The APU Science Approach.* London, HMSO.

Arbitman-Smith, R. et al (1984) Assessing cognitive change. In P.H. Brooks et al (eds) *Learning and Cognition in the Mentally Retarded.* Hillsdale, NJ, Lawrence Erlbaum Associates.

Archenhold, W.F. et al (eds) (1980) *Cognitive Development Research in Science and Mathematics.* Leeds, University of Leeds.

Ashman, A.F. (1984) Cognitive abilities of the retarded. In J.R. Kirby (ed.) *Cognitive Strategies and Educational Performance.* London, Academic Press.

Ausubel, D.P. (1968) *Educational Psychology – a Cognitive View.* New York, Holt, Rinehart & Winston.

Bannister, D. and Fransella, F. (1980) *Inquiring Man. The Psychology of Personal Constructs*, 2nd edn. Harmondsworth, Penguin.

Barker-Lunn, J.C. (1970) *Streaming in the Primary School.* Slough, NFER.

Bennett, G.K. et al (1974) *5th Manual for the Differential Aptitude Tests.* New York, Psychological Corporation.

Blackman, L.S. and Lin, A. (1984) Generalisation training in the educable mentally retarded: Intelligence and its educability revisited. In P.H. Brooks et al (eds) *Learning and Cognition in the Mentally Retarded.* Hillsdale, NJ, Lawrence Erlbaum Associates.

Bloom, B.S. (ed.) (1956) *Taxonomy of Educational Objectives. Handbook I: Cognitive Domain.* London, Longman.

Bloom, B.S. (1976) *Human Characteristics and School Learning.* New York, McGraw-Hill.

Borkowski, J.G. et al (1984) Metacognition and retardation: paradigmatic, theoretical and applied perspectives. In P.H. Brooks et al (eds) *Learning and Cognition in the Mentally Retarded.* Hillsdale, NJ, Lawrence Erlbaum Associates.

Brodie, T. (1991) Concept mapping, *School Science Review*, 73(263): 120–3.

Brooks, P.H. et al (eds) (1984) *Learning and Cognition in the Mentally Retarded.* Hillsdale, NJ, Lawrence Erlbaum Associates.

Bulman, L. (1985) *Teaching Language and Study Skills in Secondary Science.* London, Heinemann.

Byrnes, M.M. and Spitz, H.H. (1977) Performance of retarded adolescents and non-retarded children on the Tower of Hanoi problem, *American Journal of Mental Deficiency*, 81: 561–9.

Calderhead, J. (1984) *Teachers' Classroom Decision Making.* London, Holt, Rinehart & Winston.

Campione, J.C. et al (1982) Mental retardation and intelligence. In R.S. Sternberg (ed.) *Handbook of Human Intelligence.* Cambridge, Cambridge University Press.

Carr, W. and Kemmis, S. (1986) *Becoming Critical: Education, Knowledge and Action Research.* Lewes, Falmer Press.

Cattell, R.B. (1965) *The Scientific Analysis of Personality.* Harmondsworth, Penguin.

Cattell, R.B. (1970) *The Technical Handbook to the 16PF*. Illinois, Institute for Personality and Achievement Tests.

Child, D. (1981) *Psychology and the Teacher*. London, Holt, Rinehart & Winston.

Clifford, P. and Heath, A. (1984) Selection does make a difference, *Oxford Review of Education*, 10(1): 85–9.

Cohen, D. (1983) *Piaget: Critique and Reassessment*. London, Croom Helm.

Cohen, L. and Manion, L. (1981) *Perspectives on Classrooms and Schools*. London, Holt, Rinehart & Winston.

Connelly, F.M. and Clandinin, D.J. (1987) On narrative method, biography and narrative unities in the study of teaching, *Journal of Educational Thought*, 21(3): 130–9.

Cronbach, L.J. and Snow, R.E. (1977) *Aptitudes and Instructional Methods: A Handbook of Research on Interactions*. New York, Irvington.

Davies, F. and Greene, T. (1984) *Reading for Learning in the Sciences*. London, Schools Council–Oliver and Boyd.

de Charms, R. et al (1969) *Can Motives of Low Income Black Children be Changed?* St Louis, Washington University.

Denton, C. and Postlethwaite, K.C. (1985) *Able Children: Identifying them in the Classroom*. Slough, NFER–Nelson.

DES (1978) *Special Educational Needs, Report of the Committee of Enquiry into the Education of Handicapped Children and Young People* (Warnock Report). London, HMSO.

DES (1982) *Report of the Committee of Inquiry into the Teaching of Mathematics in Schools* (Cockcroft Report). London, HMSO.

DES and Welsh Office (1985a) *General Certificate of Secondary Education, The National Criteria: General Criteria*. London, HMSO.

DES and Welsh Office (1985b) *Science 5–16: A Statement of Policy*. London, HMSO.

DES and Welsh Office (1989a) *The National Curriculum. From Policy to Practice*. London, HMSO.

DES and Welsh Office (1989b) *Science in the National Curriculum*. London, HMSO.

DES and Welsh Office (1989c) *Circular 24/89 Initial Teacher Training: Approval of Courses*. London, HMSO.

DES and Welsh Office (1991a) *Technical and Vocational Educational Initiative (TVEI) England and Wales 1983–90*. London, HMSO.

DES and Welsh Office (1991b) *Science in the National Curriculum Revised Order (1991)*. London, HMSO.

Donaldson, M. (1978) *Children's Minds*. London, Fontana.

Driver, R. (1983) *The Pupil as Scientist?* Milton Keynes, Open University Press.

Driver, R. et al (eds) (1985) *Children's Ideas in Science*. Milton Keynes, Open University Press.

Employment Department (undated) *Flexible Learning: A Framework for Education and Training in the Skills Decade*. Moorfoot, Sheffield, Employment Dept.

Entwistle, N. (1981) *Styles of Learning and Teaching*. Chichester, Wiley.

Eysenck, H.J. (1953) *The Structure of Human Personality*. London, Methuen.

Eysenck, H.J. (1967) Intelligence assessment, *British Journal of Educational Psychology*, 37: 81–98.

Ferri, E. (1971) *Streaming: Two Years Later*. Slough, NFER.

Feuerstein, R. et al (1980) *Instrumental Enrichment: An Intervention Programme for Cognitive Modifiability*. Baltimore, University Park Press.

Fish, J. (1985) *Special Education: The Way Ahead*. Milton Keynes, Open University Press.

Fontana, D. (1977) *Personality and Education*. London, Open Books.

Fuchs, L.S. et al (1986) Effects of Mastery Learning procedures on student achievement, *Journal of Educational Research*, 79(5): 286–91.

Geeslin, D.H. (1984) A survey of pupil opinion concerning learning for mastery, *Education*, 105(2): 147–50.

Gagné, R.M. and Briggs, L.J. (1974) *Principles of Instructional Design*. New York, Holt, Rinehart & Winston.

Gilbert, J.K. and Osborne, R.J. (1982) Studies of pupils' alternative frameworks or misconceptions in science. In W.F. Archenhold et al (eds) *Cognitive Development Research in Science and Mathematics*. Leeds, University of Leeds.

Gilbert, J.K. and Watts, D.M. (1983) Concepts, misconceptions and alternative conceptions: changing perspectives in science education, *Studies in Science Education*, 10: 61–98.

Gray, J. and Richer, J. (1988) *Special Needs in Mainstream Schools: Classroom Responses to Learning Difficulties*. Basingstoke, Macmillan.

Guilford, J.P. (1959) Three facets of the intellect, *American Psychologist*, 14(8): 469–79.

Guilford, J.P. (1967) *The Nature of Human Intelligence*. New York, McGraw-Hill.

Guilford, J.P. (1977) *Way Beyond the IQ: Guide to Improving Intelligence and Creativity*. Buffalo, NY, Creative Education Foundation.

Guilford, J.P. (1982) Cognitive psychology's ambiguities: some suggested remedies, *Psychology Review*, 89(1): 48–59.

Guskey, T.R. and Gates, S.L. (1986) Synthesis of research on the effects of Mastery Learning in elementary and secondary classrooms, *Educational Leadership*, 43(8): 73–80.

Harrison, C. (1980) *Readability in the Classroom*. Cambridge, Cambridge University Press.

Harvey, R. et al (1982) *Mathematics Language, Learning and Teaching Series*, No. 6, M. Torbe (ed.). London, Ward Lock.

Hashweh, M.Z. (1986) Toward an explanation of conceptual change, *European Journal of Science Education*, 8(3): 229–49.

Hirst, P.H. and Peters, R.S. (1970) *The Logic of Education*. London, Routledge & Kegan Paul.

HMI (1978) *Mixed Ability Work in Comprehensive Schools*. London, HMSO.

HMI (1979) *Aspects of Secondary Education*. London, HMSO.

HMI (1982) *The New Teacher in School*. London, HMSO.

Howard, R.W. (1987) *Concepts and Schemata: An Introduction*. London, Cassell Education.

Howarth, R. (1985) personal communication.

Kelley, H.H. (1972) Causal schemata and the attribution process. In E.E. Jones et al (eds) *Attribution: Perceiving the Causes of Behaviour*. Morristown, NJ, General Learning Press.

Kelly, G. (1955) *The Psychology of Personal Constructs*, Vols 1 and 2. New York, Norton.

Kerslake, D. (1982) Talking about mathematics. In R. Harvey et al (eds) *Language Teaching and Learning: Mathematics*. London, Ward Lock Educational.

Lavin, D.E. (1965) *The Prediction of Academic Performance*. New York, Russell Sage Foundation.

Louden, W. (1991) *Understanding Teaching – Continuity and Change in Teachers' Knowledge*. London, Cassell Educational.

Lunzer, E. and Gardner, K. (1984) *Learning from the Written Word*. London, Schools Council–Heinemann.

Lupart, J. and Mulcahy, R. (1984) Some thoughts on research in learning disabilities and attention. In J.R. Kirby (ed.) *Cognitive Strategies and Educational Performance*. London, Academic Press.

McClelland, D.C. (1955) *Studies in Motivation*. New York, Appleton-Century-Crofts.

McClelland, D.C. (1973) Testing for competence rather than 'intelligence', *American Psychologist*, 28: 1–14.

McClelland, D.C. and Winter, D.G. (1969) *Motivating Economic Achievement*. New York, The Free Press.

McIntyre, D. (1988) Designing a teacher education curriculum from theory and research on teacher knowledge. In J. Calderhead (ed.) *Teachers' Professional Learning*. Lewes, Falmer Press.

McIntyre, D. and Postlethwaite, K. (1989) Attending to individual differences: a conceptual analysis. In N. Jones (ed.) *Special Educational Needs Review*, Vol. 2. London, Falmer Press.

Male, J. and Thompson, C. (1985) *The Educational Implications of Disability: A Guide for Teachers*. London, RADAR.

Mogdil, S. and Mogdil C. (eds) (1982) *Jean Piaget, Consensus and Controversy*. London, Holt, Rinehart & Winston.

Montgomery, D. (1990) *Special Needs in Ordinary Schools: Children with Learning Difficulties*. London, Cassell Educational.

National Curriculum Council (1989a) *Circular 5: Implementing the National Curriculum – Participation by Pupils with Special Educational Needs*. York, NCC.

National Curriculum Council (1989b) *A Curriculum for All*. York, NCC.

National Curriculum Council (1991) *Science and Pupils with Special Educational Needs: A Workshop Pack for Key Stages 1 & 2*. York, NCC.

Newbold, D. (1977) *Ability Grouping – The Banbury Enquiry*. Slough, NFER.

Nussbaum, J. and Novick, S. (1981) Brainstorming in the classroom to invent a model: a case study, *School Science Review*, 62: 771–8.

Ormerod, M.B. and Duckworth, D. (1975) *Pupils' Attitudes to Science*. Slough, NFER.

Osborne, R.J. et al (1983) Science teaching and children's views of the world, *European Journal of Science Education*, 5(1): 1–14.

Osborne, R. and Freyberg, P. (1985) *Learning in Science The Implications of Children's Science*. Auckland, Heinemann.

Pask, G. (1975) *The Cybernetics of Human Learning and Performance*. London, Hutchinson.

Perera, K. (1980) The assessment of linguistic difficulty in reading material, *Education Review*, 32(2): 151–61.

Perera, K. (1986) Some Linguistic difficulties in school subjects. In B. Gillham (ed.) *The Language of School Subjects*. London, Heinemann.

Posner, G.J. et al (1982) Accommodation of a scientific conception: toward a theory of conceptual change, *Science Education*, 66: 211–27.

Postlethwaite, K.C. (1984) Teacher-based Identification of Pupils with High Potential in Physics and English, DPhil thesis, University of Oxford.

Postlethwaite, K. and Denton, C. (1978) *Streams for the Future?* Banbury, Pubansco.

Postlethwaite, K.C. and Jaspars, J.M.F. (1986) The experimental use of personal constructs in educational research: the critical triad procedure, *British Journal of Educational Psychology*, 56: 241–54.

Postlethwaite, K.C. and Hackney, A.C. (1988) *Special Needs in Mainstream Schools, Organising a School's Response*. Basingstoke, Macmillan.

Postlethwaite, K.C. and Reynolds, R.D. (1990) *TVEI in Initial Teacher Education: A Report on the Activities of the TEIV in Balanced Science Syndicate*. Reading, University of Reading.

Powell, R. (1991) *Resources for Flexible Learning*. Stafford, Network Educational Press.

Raban, B. and Postlethwaite, K. (1988) *Special Needs in Mainstream Schools: Classroom Responses to Learning Difficulties*. Basingstoke, Macmillan Education.

Raviv, A. et al (1980) Causal perceptions of success and failure by advantaged, integrated and disadvantaged pupils, *British Journal of Educational Psychology*, 50: 137–46.

Raynor, J.O. (1970) Relationships between achievement – related motives, future orientation, and academic performance, *Journal of Personality and Social Psychology*, 15: 28–33.

Renzulli, J.S. (1977) *The Enrichment Triad Model: A guide for Developing Defensible Programs for the Gifted and Talented*. Connecticut, Creative Learning Press.

Ross, L.E. and Ross, S.M. (1981) The visual scanning and fixation behaviour of the retarded. In N. Ellis (ed.) *International Review of Research in Mental Retardation*, Vol. 10. New York, Academic Press.

Schiff, M. and Lewontin, R. (1986) *Education and Class: the Irrelevance of IQ in Genetic Studies*. Oxford, Clarendon Press.

Schön, D. (1983) *The Reflective Practitioner*. New York, Basic Books.

Schön, D. (1987) *Educating the Reflective Practitioner*. San Francisco, Jossey-Bass.

Seiber, J. et al (1977) *Anxiety, Learning and Instruction*. Hillsdale, NJ, Lawrence Erlbaum Associates.

Selley, N.J. (1981) The place of alternative models in school science, *School Science Review* (December): 252–9.

Shayer, M. and Adey, P. (1981) *Towards a Science of Science Teaching*. London, Heinemann Educational.

Shayer, M. and Beasley, F. (1987) Does instrumental enrichment work? *British Educational Research Journal*, 13(2): 101–19.

Sperber, R. and McCauley, C. (1984) Semantic processing efficiency in the mentally retarded. In P.H. Brooks et al (eds) *Learning and Cognition in the Mentally Retarded*. Hillsdale, NJ, Lawrence Erlbaum Associates.

Sternberg, R.S. (1984) Macrocomponents and microcomponents of intelligence: some proposed loci of mental retardation. In P.H. Brooks et al (eds) *Learning and Cognition in the Mentally Retarded*. Hillsdale, NJ, Lawrence Erlbaum Associates.

Sternberg, R.S. (1985) *Beyond IQ: A Triarchic Theory of Human Intelligence*. Cambridge, Cambridge University Press.

Sternberg, R.S. (1988) Intelligence. In R.S. Sternberg and E.E. Smith (eds) *The Psychology of Human Thought*. Cambridge University Press.

Tannenbaum, A.J. (1983) *Gifted Children: Psychological and Educational Perspectives*. New York, Macmillan.

Thurstone, L.L. (1938) Primary mental abilities, *Psychological Monographs*, I.

Vernon, P.E. (1957) *Secondary School Selection*. London, Methuen.

Vincent, D. et al (1983) *A Review of Reading Tests*. Windsor, NFER–Nelson.

Waterhouse, P. (1983) *Managing the Learning Process*. London, McGraw-Hill.

Watts, M. and Bentley, D. (1987) Constructivism in the classroom: enabling conceptual change by words and deeds, *British Educational Research Journal*, 13(2): 121.

Weber, K.J. (1974) *Yes, They Can!* Milton Keynes, Open University Press.

Weiner, B. (1976) Motivation. In W.K. Estes (ed.) *Handbook of Learning and Cognitive Processes*. Vol. 3, *Approaches to Human Learning and Motivation*. Hillsdale, NJ, Lawrence Erlbaum Associates.

Weiner, B. (1985) *Human Motivation*. New York, Springer-Verlag.

Weller, K. and Craft, A. (1983) *Making Up Our Minds: An Exploratory Study of Instrumental Enrichment*. London, Schools Council.

Wilson, J.B. (1975) *Educational Theory and the Preparation of Teachers*. Slough, NFER.

Witkin, H.A. et al (1977) Field-dependent and field-independent cognitive styles and their educational implications, *Review of Educational Research*, 14(1): 1–64.

Wood, R. and Napthali, N.A. (1975) Assessment in the classroom: What do teachers look for? *Educational Studies*, 1(3): 151–61.

Zigler, E. and Seitz, V. (1982) Social policy and intelligence. In R.S. Sternberg (ed.) *Handbook of Human Intelligence*. Cambridge, Cambridge University Press.

INDEX